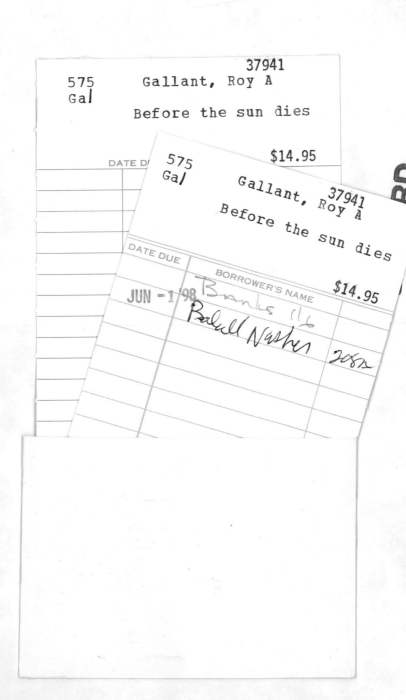

37941

575
Gal

Gallant, Roy A

Before the sun dies

$14.95

DATE DUE

575
Gal

Gallant, Roy A   37941

Before the sun dies

$14.95

DATE DUE	BORROWER'S NAME	
JUN -1 '98	*Branks 16*	
	Badal Nather	*208n*

BEFORE THE SUN DIES

The Story of Evolution

ROY A. GALLANT

Also by Roy A. Gallant

RAINBOWS, MIRAGES, AND SUNDOGS: The Sky as a
    Source of Wonder

PRIVATE LIVES OF THE STARS

THE MACMILLAN BOOK OF ASTRONOMY

101 QUESTIONS AND ANSWERS ABOUT THE UNIVERSE

THE PLANETS: Exploring the Solar System

MEMORY: How It Works and How To Improve It

THE CONSTELLATIONS: How They Came To Be

EARTH'S CHANGING CLIMATE

BEYOND EARTH: The Search for Extraterrestrial Life

HOW LIFE BEGAN: Creation vs. Evolution

FIRES IN THE SKY: The Birth and Death of Stars

BEFORE THE SUN DIES

The Story of Evolution

ROY A. GALLANT

MACMILLAN PUBLISHING COMPANY
New York

COLLIER MACMILLAN PUBLISHERS
London

For Ginny and Bob

Macmillan Publishing Company
866 Third Avenue, New York, NY 10022
Collier Macmillan Canada, Inc.
First Edition
Printed in the United States of America

10 9 8 7 6 5 4 3 2 1

The text of this book is set in 12 point Garamond No. 3.

Library of Congress Cataloging-in-Publication Data
Gallant, Roy A.
Before the sun dies : the story of evolution / Roy A. Gallant.—1st ed.
p.   cm. Bibliography: p. Includes index.
Summary: Presents the theories, controversies, and latest
scientific thinking on how the Solar System, the Earth, and the
first biological organisms came to be and how the latter changed and
adapted for survival. Includes a glossary of terms.
ISBN 0-02-735771-6
1. Evolution—Juvenile literature. [1. Evolution.] I. Title.
QH367.1G35 1989 575—dc 19   88-8284 CIP AC

ACKNOWLEDGMENTS

I wish to thank Dr. Edward J. Kormondy, friend, biologist, and chancellor of the University of Hawaii—Hilo, for reading the manuscript of this book for technical accuracy. I would also like to thank Dr. Henry Albers, friend, colleague, and astronomer at Vassar College, Poughkeepsie, New York, for reading those sections of the book describing Earth's history as a planet. My thanks also to Four Winds Press (an imprint of Macmillan Publishing Company) for permission to adapt for this book brief excerpts from my book, *Earth's Changing Climate,* copyright © 1979 by Roy A. Gallant.

What Is Evolution?

"The word evolution is commonly associated with evolving plants and animals, nothing else. It suggests changes in the biological world. . . . Yet for a century scientists have been aware of evolution beyond the biological kingdom. We have seen that volcanic action and the oxidizing of lava rocks indicate that this planet's surface still changes with time; it evolves, and our atmosphere does also. The variety among stars suggests stellar evolution. For half a century we have realized that the fact that our Sun is shining is evidence that it is steadily losing mass-energy . . . and therefore that it is evolving. Similarly, therefore, star shine must mean stellar evolution, a much mightier operation than we can muster among the animals and plants and noncellular organisms on the Earth's surface. It is only a short step from stellar evolution to galaxy evolution. Going further, we see that the discovery of the expanding Universe indicates that growth, change, evolution affect also the future of the galaxy of galaxies."

Harlow Shapley, from
Beyond the Observatory

Foreword

The word evolution arouses different thoughts and reactions in different people. Some immediately think of the dinosaurs, woolly mammoths, dodo birds, and other animals that became extinct thousands or millions of years ago. Sometimes it is not hard to understand how certain animal and plant species become extinct. People move in and cut down a forest or drain a marsh, and so deprive one or more animal species of shelter and food. Other times it is not easy to understand why a certain species, or an entire group of closely related species, becomes extinct. The dinosaurs are an example. Biologists continue to try to solve that puzzle. Was it a slow onset of climate change that gradually killed off the dinosaurs, or was it a sudden event such as the explosion of a giant comet or asteroid? Such a catastrophic event could have enclosed the planet in a dust cloud causing severe climate change by blocking out energy from the Sun.

While it is interesting to speculate and wonder about the countless number of times animal and plant species have become extinct in the dim past, it is even more interesting to wonder how those species came into being in the first place. The English naturalist Charles Darwin was among the first to ponder that question and suggest an answer based on solid scientific grounds. His answer was evolution through natural selection. Since Darwin developed the principle of evolution in the mid-1800s, many other scientists the world over have spent their lives studying how animal and plant species evolve, or change, into new species in a seemingly endless process that began more than three billion years ago, and that continues to this day. That evolution has occurred in the past, and is occurring today, is a well-established fact. But the forces that drive evolution are sometimes hard to pinpoint. However, scientists continue to gather evidence that supports the fact of evolution, and they continue to reveal ways in which species evolve.

Evolution is a process that involves change. A pond changes gradually into a marsh or swamp and eventually becomes dry land with shrubs and trees. A star is born out of a cloud of dust and gas that heats up and shines for a few billion years as a Sun. It then ends its evolution as a dark, cold object. While that star pours energy off into space and bathes its system of planets in sunshine, populations of organisms on one or more of those planets change in response to changes in the environment. Over periods measured in millions of years, millions of different kinds of microbes, plants, and animals come into being and become extinct amid endless change.

While change is one key to evolution, time is another. Biological time is relatively short, measured in the lifetime of a human, an elephant, or a bristlecone pine tree, which may live more than a thousand years. Evolutionary time is relatively long, measured in tens of thousands, millions, and billions of years, as in the life spans of certain species and of stars.

It is hard for the human mind to grasp the immensity of evolutionary time. Although we can experience the passing of our own personal time, we cannot experience the passage of evolutionary time. We can examine the fossil footprints of great lumbering creatures that roamed the forests of the past. Scientists can crush and analyze pieces of the rock containing those footprints and say that the rock is 200 million years old, and so the creature that left its footprints in the mud that turned into that rock also must have lived at least 200 million years ago.

In the pages that follow, science writer Roy Gallant has told the story of evolution clearly, convincingly, and in a way that is bound to capture the imaginations of readers young and old alike. As the story unfolds and you read on, let your mind be stretched as you discover many of the marvelously exciting evolutionary changes that have occurred on this planet since it was formed more than 4 billion years ago.

Edward J. Kormondy
Chancellor, University of Hawaii—Hilo
West Oahu College
Hilo, Hawaii

Contents

Chemicals are interchangeable between inorganic
and organic things and thereby unify the
nonliving and living worlds at the atomic and
molecular levels. Living things are not made of
sacred substances that require special creation
in a nonliving material world.
— *Edward R. Harrison, 1981*

1

When Is a Thing
a "Living" Thing?

MATTER AND ORDER

Compared to an atom you are huge, but compared to a galaxy you are
tiny. Can you think of a way that you, atoms, and galaxies are alike?
One thing the three of you have in common is an orderliness of your
matter. Another thing is energy, which keeps your matter orderly.

Of the more than one hundred different kinds of atoms, each has
a fixed number of atomic building blocks: bits of matter called electrons,
protons, and neutrons. The simplest atom of all is the most plentiful
one in the universe—hydrogen. It has a single proton at the center and
a single electron held at a certain distance from the proton by electrical
forces.

What about the orderliness of the collection of atoms that is you?
Your body contains millions of hydrogen atoms, along with more complex atoms of oxygen, nitrogen, phosphorous, carbon, potassium, and

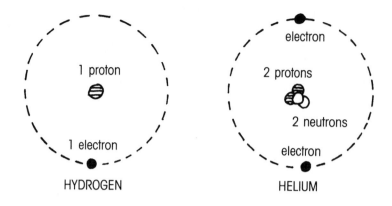

Hydrogen and helium are the two simplest of the more than one hundred chemical elements and make up nearly all of the matter in the universe.

sodium, for example. All of these atoms are arranged in a certain orderly fashion and are made to work together as a human being. The work is done by electrical energy that makes your nerves send messages throughout your body; by chemical energy that digests the food you eat; and by the mechanical energy of your muscles that enables you to walk, pedal a bicycle, or turn the pages of this book.

What about the orderliness of a galaxy? The hundreds of billions of stars, planets and their moons, comets, and gas and dust between the stars that form a galaxy also are made up of atoms. In a galaxy there are the same kinds of atoms that are in you, and many other kinds as well—uranium, argon, gold, and silver, for example. Gravitational energy is what holds a galaxy together and keeps it orderly. Gravity also keeps the Solar System orderly by holding the planets and their moons in orbit around the Sun instead of letting them fly off into space in every which direction.

No one can deny that nonliving and living things both are made up of atoms. But where did the atoms of our bodies, the planets, and trillions upon trillions of stars come from? Astronomers tell us that the lightweight hydrogen atoms were fashioned some 15 billion years ago, moments after the Big Bang explosion that started the universe. All the

Galaxies are the largest known single units of matter in the universe. From a great distance in space our home galaxy, the Milky Way, would resemble the Andromeda Galaxy (shown here) some 2 million light-years distant. The two bright objects are smaller companion galaxies. The smaller dots are stars belonging to our galaxy.

heavier atoms of our bodies—such as carbon, nitrogen, and iron—were formed in the cores of gigantic stars that blew themselves to bits as supernovas about 5 billion years ago. While living things are born and die, their atoms, which they have borrowed from nature for a time, are virtually ageless. When people and other living things die, their atoms gradually are released into the soil and to the air where they are available for use again.

Some 90 percent of the atoms in the universe are hydrogen, as are most of the atoms of our bodies. Our hydrogen atoms are joined to oxygen atoms and form molecules of a watery fluid that bathes our body tissues and helps to keep us alive. Our skin is simply a bag that keeps the watery fluid from leaking out.

The carbon atoms of our bodies also join with atoms of the elements hydrogen, nitrogen, oxygen, phosphorus, and sulfur to make molecules of many other substances that we need in order to stay alive. Among those substances are protein building blocks required for growth and the repair of damaged body parts. Other molecules store and release energy that drives the many chemical reactions that take place in our bodies all the time we are alive.

Those six elements are present in all living things—from the tiniest bacteria to the largest whales. Drained of their watery fluids, the weight of *all* living things is 99 percent hydrogen, carbon, nitrogen, oxygen, phosphorus, and sulfur. So atoms of certain kinds, and in certain amounts in relation to each other, are common to all things said to be "living" but are not common to rocks, clouds, and other things said to be "nonliving."

WHAT IS LIFE?

Ask someone to define "life" and the person will probably list some of the things a living thing does rather than what it is made of—it moves around, it grows, it reproduces more of its kind, and eventually it dies. Surely an atom and a galaxy are not alive since they don't do any of those things, except move around.

What about a seed that just sits on a shelf for a hundred years? Is it alive during that time it isn't growing? If the seed is planted and watered, its cells begin to divide and it develops into a full-grown plant. Then there is no doubt about its being alive. One-thousand-year-old seeds of bristlecone pine trees have been planted and "brought to life" after their long period of inactivity. Was the seed alive during that time? Drop a dry yeast tablet into a cup of water and you get instant life in the form of millions of living and active yeast cells. Was the yeast alive when stored in a box on the shelf? Human cells can be frozen and stored for many years. Sperm cells, which are male sex cells, are an example. When thawed and properly cared for, they resume living. Were those cells dead during the time they were frozen? Or was a process of earlier activity merely interrupted for a while and then restarted?

When we try to answer the question of what makes living things different from nonliving things, the answer must include everything that we think of as being "alive." According to the paleontologist Niles Eldredge, of New York's American Museum of Natural History, "If we can specify the several fundamental aspects of living systems common to them all, we will more than likely also be outlining the general conditions that originally had to be met for life to have sprung from nonliving matter. And once we have done *that,* we have provided ourselves with a key to unraveling the history of life from its inception, well over 3 billion years ago, right up to the present moment."

LIFE IS WHAT MATTER DOES

So far, we have said that certain kinds of atoms in certain amounts make up all matter said to be living. We can now add the activity of that matter to the definition. So when we talk about life, it is important to consider the way in which the atoms and molecules of living matter react with one another and with atoms and molecules outside of the living system.

A living thing as complex as a human or an elephant or a giant redwood tree stays alive and expresses its aliveness by endlessly organizing and reorganizing its billions of atoms from one moment to the next. That is something a piece of quartz, however well ordered its atoms may be, cannot do. Consider what happens when you eat a piece of apple pie. The molecules of the chunks of apple in the pie are organized in a way typical of an apple, at least they were before the apple was cooked. When you digest that apple matter, certain chemicals of your body break down the apple matter and reorganize it into people matter and into molecules that store energy. That part of the apple matter that your body can't use is later discarded as waste.

The smallest unit of life is the cell. Most cells are much smaller than the dot over this letter *i*. Yet the tiniest cell is able to carry out all

The cell is the smallest unit of life and contains many parts that carry out special functions. In an animal cell, the cell membrane separates the cell proper from the outside environment but permits the exchange of materials with the environment. The nucleus is the control center for the cell. Mitochondria serve as a power supply. Ribosomes are the sites where new protein is made, aided by the action of nucleoli, and Golgi bodies are involved with cell secretions. Protoplasm is a watery living substance present within both the cell and its nucleus. Cells have many other structures not shown here.

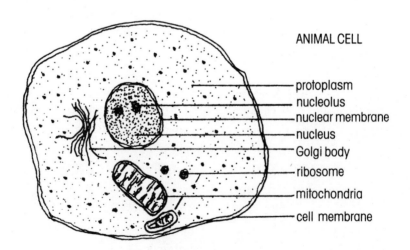

ANIMAL CELL

- protoplasm
- nucleolus
- nuclear membrane
- nucleus
- Golgi body
- ribosome
- mitochondria
- cell membrane

of the basic life functions, and that is why a single cell is such a remarkable thing, not because it is so small. It feeds, rids itself of waste matter, grows, repairs its damaged parts, and produces more cells like itself. Your body is made up of some 10 quadrillion (10,000,000,000,000,000) cells of about one hundred different kinds. Just as you have a stomach, brain, kidney, and other organs that keep you alive, a cell has special parts, each carrying out certain functions that keep the cell alive and healthy. If one of those parts is damaged and the damage is not major, the cell repairs itself by selecting from outside itself the kinds and numbers of atoms and molecules it needs for repair. The cell then makes new molecules to repair itself. That also is remarkable.

Cells function and maintain themselves for as long as they are able to keep their atoms and molecules organized. *Organized* is a key word when we speak of living matter. From a cell's point of view the outside world is a disorderly collection of atoms and molecules. As your fluid body is protected from the harsh (dry) outside world by your skin, a cell's protection against the harsh (disorderly) outside world is a membrane sac. Without that membrane, the orderly arrangement of the cell's parts would be lost, and the cell would die instantly.

A cell's membrane does not completely cut the cell off from its outside environment. All over the membrane are tiny openings. These windows on the outside world let certain molecules enter the cell when they are needed. The windows also let waste molecules within the cell be removed. So there is a continual two-way flow of materials entering and leaving a cell as the cell exchanges matter with its outside environment.

Keeping certain kinds and amounts of molecules inside itself, taking in nutrient molecules, ridding itself of waste molecules, repairing itself if damaged, making more cells of its own pattern, and maintaining its orderly society of molecules against the chaotic outside world—these, then, are the activities carried out by the simplest unit of life of which all living things are composed. They are also the activities of all other living matter—from aardvarks to zebras.

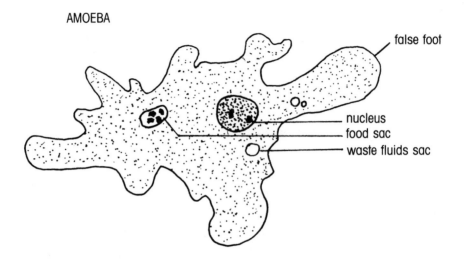

AMOEBA

false foot

nucleus
food sac
waste fluids sac

An amoeba is an independent cell that carries out all life functions. It is a mass of protoplasm contained within a cell membrane that stretches this way and that. To move, the amoeba simply flows into a bulge in its cell membrane called a "false foot." It engulfs food particles, then stores and "eats" them in food sacs (vacuoles). Its fluid wastes are collected in fluid vacuoles that move out of the cell by passing through the membrane.

So, on one level, we can regard "life" as an activity, or process, of the right mix of chemicals reacting with the environment. That right mix might be in the form of a rooster or a mosquito or a single cell, such as an amoeba. All have those characteristics we collectively call "life." They include

1. the ability to protect itself within a membrane that acts as a defense against the disorderly outside world;

2. a process, involving energy, that drives the many chemical activities that make new parts, repair worn or damaged parts, and generally maintain the organism from one minute to the next;

3. a way of obtaining matter and energy from the outside environment and using that matter and energy for growth and maintenance;

4. and a way of reproducing more organisms like itself.

All organisms of a single kind, such as dogs, cats, white birch trees, or people are said to belong to a certain species. Human beings, for instance, belong to the species *Homo sapiens* while cats belong to the species *Felis catus.* We can define a species as any population whose individual members look pretty much alike, who can produce offspring, and whose offspring in turn can have offspring.

Over long periods of time a species may change, or evolve, into new species. Or all members of a species may die, in which case the species becomes extinct, which is what happened to the many species of the dinosaurs some 65 million years ago. Of all the species of animals and plants that have ever lived on Earth, 99.99 percent are now extinct. However, life itself has gone on uninterrupted as new species have evolved and replaced the ones that became extinct.

Sometimes extinctions occur quietly and go unnoticed. Other times they are catastrophic. As we will learn in a later chapter, there have been several single catastrophic events that have shaken Earth in the past, and each has wiped out at least 95 percent of all living species. That is an impressive figure when you consider that about 2 million species of animals and nearly 1 million species of plants have been identified. Some biologists think there may be as many as 30 million living species of animals and plants combined!

When scientists study the ways in which living matter has evolved since it first appeared on Earth nearly 4 billion years ago, they examine life at many different levels—at the level of cells; at the level of whole organisms, whether trees or turtles; at the level of populations of those organisms; and at the level of communities of different kinds of organisms and how they affect one another.

EVOLUTION: A BROAD VIEW

But scientists want a still broader view of evolution in the universe. Evolution is not restricted to living matter only. Practically everything around us evolves—the atmosphere, mountains, the language we speak, Earth as a planet, and the stars. It is remarkable to learn that 99 percent of all known matter in the universe is still in the simple stage of evolution, that of disorganized atoms of the two oldest and simplest elements—hydrogen and helium. That leaves only 1 percent of all the matter produced by the Big Bang organized as stars, planets, and the living matter those planets support. Disorder seems to be the rule in the universe with the organized matter of stars, planets, and living systems being the exception.

Astronomers study stellar evolution, or how the vast amounts of hydrogen and helium became organized as stars and what happens to these stars throughout their life spans of a few million or a few billion years. In addition to wanting to understand how stars—and galaxies—evolve, they want to know how the universe of galaxies is evolving now. Our telescopes show us that all the billions upon billions of galaxies appear to be rushing away from one another in a universe that is expanding. What will the future hold for the universe? Will it just keep on expanding forever? Or will the galaxies one day slow down and the universe begin to fall back in on itself and produce another Big Bang that will start things all over again?

When biologists speak of evolution, they use the expression "organic" evolution, which refers only to living matter. But eventually they must consider the universe of nonliving matter as well because it is that very matter that became the stuff of all the living forms known to us.

With the Sun as a source of energy, nonliving matter on Earth was organized first into the simplest living matter by a process of chemical evolution. Then over 3.8 billion years that first living matter—in the form of bacteria—underwent a process of biological evolution that produced all the complex life forms known to us.

Biological evolution on the scale that has occurred on Earth needs a lot of time. It is impossible for the mind to grasp the meaning of a million or a billion years of evolution. If it helps, let each page of this book represent one year. A billion years would be represented by a stack of these books, without their covers, 50 miles high.

Not only did biological evolution need a long time to give rise to the assortment of complex plants and animals known to us, but just the right conditions on our planet were also needed for the process of chemical and biological evolution to begin—the right kinds of chemical raw materials, the right environmental conditions, and the energy to manipulate that matter.

Whether or not we are alone in the universe as complex living matter capable of making statements and asking questions about ourselves, we do not know. It is hard to imagine that we are, but this is getting ahead of our story of evolution and is a topic we will return to in the last chapter.

*Who would deny that such bodies {as planets}, floating
everywhere in the universal space, do not leave behind
them the germs of life wherever the planetary conditions
are already suitable to promote creation?*
—Herman Von Helmholtz, 1884

2

A Place for Earth

STARTING WITH A BIG BANG

It must have been the most fantastic explosion anyone can imagine.
What was to become every piece of matter in the universe was packed
into a tiny pinpoint of mass, a gigantic superatom. Sometime between
12 billion and 20 billion years ago, to the best of our knowledge, that
superatom exploded in what astronomers call the Big Bang.

The fireball explosion sent energy and matter hurling off in all
directions, launching an evolutionary course of expansion. At that moment, time, the universe, and evolution began. The universe has been
growing larger ever since. Evidence for such a furiously hot beginning
for the universe comes in a fossil form of heat detected by radio telescopes.

HYDROGEN AND THE FORMATION OF GALAXIES

Just after the explosion, nearly all the universe was a hot and tightly
packed cloud of hydrogen. The large number of hydrogen atoms packed
tightly together meant lots of collisions among the atoms, and the great
heat caused the collisions to be violent. Over the next several seconds,
many of the hydrogen atoms joined, fusing into atoms of helium, just
as happens today in the hot cores of stars. Then over the next minute

or so of expansion the hydrogen atoms cooled and spread out too thinly for more atomic fusions to take place. So in the few minutes after the universe began, the only chemistry possible involved only hydrogen and helium, the two simplest chemical elements. Nine out of every ten atoms making up the universe were hydrogen and one was helium.

We now move forward in time to about 100,000 to a million years after the Big Bang. Because of the wild nature of the expanding matter, it was not spread evenly through space. Instead, the mixture of hydrogen and helium collected into huge loosely packed clouds. These clouds were the early stages of the galaxies, those vast cities of stars we see throughout space today. We can imagine some parts of a galaxy-cloud having large and dense collections of hydrogen and helium while others had only small amounts of matter. The galaxies probably took about a billion years to form, sometime from about 10 billion to 15 billion years ago. So some 12 or so billion years ago our home galaxy was a newly formed collection of hydrogen and helium gas.

THE FORMATION OF STARS

As soon as galaxies began to form, so did stars, as they continue to form by the millions to this day. Each new galaxy cloud contained millions of smaller cloud clumps of hydrogen sprinkled with helium. These smaller clouds—many millions of miles across—became the birthplace of stars. We can imagine some of the bigger clouds with lots of matter, or mass, attracting and swallowing up less massive clouds nearby. The more massive a cloud, the stronger its gravity and its ability to pull surrounding matter into itself.

Although no one knows what gravity is, we know how it works. For example, the more massive any two objects are, the stronger their gravitational attraction for each other. And the closer any two objects are, the stronger their attraction for each other. So large objects in space near each other, such as two galaxies, attract each other more strongly than smaller objects far apart, such as two planets located at opposite ends of the Milky Way.

As a hydrogen star-cloud became more and more massive by gravitationally sweeping up more matter, its gravity caused the matter to tumble in toward the core region where it packed itself tighter and tighter. In this way, the star began to contract. As greater amounts of hydrogen became packed into the core region, the pressure there kept increasing because of the weight of upper layers of hydrogen tumbling in and pressing on the core region. As the infall of matter continued, the star-cloud took on the shape of an immense ball. It had become a protostar.

Lots of pressure produces lots of heat. Because the core regions of the newly forming stars were packed more tightly with gas than the surface regions were, the cores heated up more. For example, the core gases of the Sun today are more than two thousand times hotter than the surface gases. As the core temperature of a typical young protostar continued to heat up, eventually the young star became hot enough to glow a dull red. The continued sweeping up and gravitational infall of still more hydrogen sent the core temperature high enough to make the protostar begin to shine a bright cherry red. Still later, when the temperature reached about 10 million degrees (called kelvins), the core of the young star was like the universe right after the Big Bang. There was enough heat and densely packed hydrogen atoms for the atoms to fuse into helium (see box on facing page). After about 100 million years, this new source of energy caused the star to shine with a still hotter yellowish white light.

The Sun is just such a star today, fusing hydrogen into helium. Its core temperature of about 15 million kelvins is hot enough to heat the surface gases to about 6,000 kelvins and emit a yellowish white light.

THE EVOLUTION OF STARS

On any clear night binoculars will reveal that stars come in many colors—red, yellow, and blue white, for instance. Their colors are keys to their temperatures. A star that forms out of a hydrogen cloud with only about one-tenth as much matter as the Sun has cannot raise its core temperature

Nuclear Fusion: Changing Matter into Energy

As the temperature of the hydrogen gas in the core of a protostar is raised higher and higher, something interesting happens to the hydrogen atoms. At about 300 kelvins (room temperature) whole atoms dart about and bounce off one another. Raise the temperature to 10,000 kelvins and the atoms begin to collide so forcefully that their electrons are knocked away. We then end up with free electrons swimming about in a sea of free protons, all bumping into one another and bouncing away.

If we raise the temperature still more—to about 10 million kelvins—something interesting also happens to the protons. They are now darting about so fast and colliding so vigorously that their invisible energy bumpers no longer work, and two protons may fuse into a single lump of matter. As they do, part of their mass is changed into energy. The single lump next fuses with another free proton, and another tiny burst of energy is given off. A series of such fusions eventually builds the nucleus of a helium atom, and at each step along the way a little bit of proton mass is changed into energy. That, in brief, is how a star like the Sun shines and releases energy.

to much more than 10 million kelvins. Such stars do not produce much energy in their cores and so are rather small and cool red stars, called red dwarfs. The core of a star that forms out of a hydrogen cloud with about ten times more matter than the Sun's star-cloud heats up to about 50 million kelvins. These extremely hot stars shine with a bluish white light and are very much larger than the Sun. We call them blue giants and supergiants. They are the real superstars of the universe.

In the past few decades astronomers have been able to learn something about the evolution of stars. Today they know that the life span of a star is set by the amount of hydrogen that was in the star's original star-cloud. Hydrogen in the core region of any star is the fuel that keeps the star shining. For as long as there is hydrogen to be fused into helium, the star keeps shining. When the hydrogen fuel is gone, a star enters its death stage.

Low-mass stars such as the red dwarfs use up their hydrogen fuel very slowly. That is why they are cool and feeble emitters of energy and have a life span of perhaps trillions of years. More massive and energetic stars such as the Sun use up their hydrogen faster and have a life span of about 10 billion years. The blue giant stars are the most energetic, and although they have huge stores of hydrogen mass, they use it up so fast that they have a life span of only tens of thousands of years.

During their lives, stars are the element factories of the universe. The kinds of elements they produce are determined by how massive they are. Red dwarf stars do not become hot enough to produce elements heavier than helium. Medium-mass stars such as the Sun run a more complex course of evolution. When their hydrogen supply is all but gone, energy production in the core slows and the core pressure lowers. A lower core pressure allows the material just above the core to tumble inward. The result of this sudden infall of matter is an increase in temperature and pressure. Both are pushed so high that the helium that had been building up over billions of years now fuses into still heavier atoms, in this case carbon. Very massive stars can produce still heavier elements such as oxygen, then silicon, and finally iron. Elements heavier than iron cannot be produced in average stars such as the Sun, only in supernova explosions.

How will the Sun evolve over the remaining 5 billion years of its total life span of some 10 billion years? In about 5 billion years we can expect it to exhaust its hydrogen fuel supply. The core will then collapse and send the temperature and pressure soaring, resulting in a new outburst of energy. The outburst of energy will cause the Sun to swell up and become an enormous red giant star, at which time it will be so large that it will engulf Mercury and Venus. (At the present time the Sun is large enough so that one hundred Earths could be lined up across the

Sun's equator.) The Sun will be emitting enough energy to boil away Earth's oceans and melt the surface rocks down to a soup of glowing molten rock. During its red giant stage of several million years, the Sun will produce elements heavier than helium by fusing helium into those heavier elements. When it no longer has the ability to produce new fusions, the nuclear furnace in the Sun's core will be shut down forever. The Sun will collapse once again. But this time it will just keep on collapsing until it is only about the size of Earth, or smaller.

The Sun's energy output will then come only from the tightly packed material around the slowly cooling core. Because there will be such a small surface area from which the star's dwindling store of energy can be emitted, the Sun will become an intensely white object called a white dwarf. No white dwarf star can go on radiating energy forever, since no new energy is being produced in the core. Gradually, over another period of several billion years, the white-dwarf Sun will be destined to cool and give off less and less energy. Eventually its light will fade, and it will become an object that can best be described as a black dwarf.

So the evolution of a star like the Sun is 1) from an immense cloud of cool gas that collapses into a sphere that heats up enough to fuse hydrogen into helium, 2) to a star that shines more or less steadily for perhaps 10 billion years, 3) to a red giant, 4) to a white dwarf, and finally 5) to a dead black dwarf.

SUPERNOVAS: THE HEAVY-ELEMENT FACTORIES

The most massive stars are supergiants some thirty times more massive than the Sun. They produce so much energy that they shine with a blue white light. When one of these stars has nearly exhausted its hydrogen fuel, the core cools a bit, shrinks, and allows the overlying gases to fall inward. The core is squeezed with crushing force in a vise of gravity. Temperatures keep rising and many different fusions take place until the core becomes mostly iron. As a normal shining star, the supergiant cannot produce elements heavier than iron, even though its core temperature is now about a billion kelvins. It has reached the critical stage of its life.

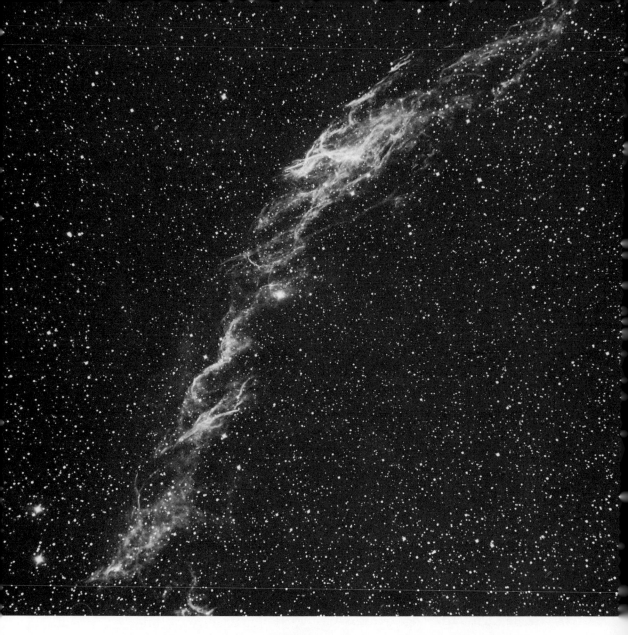

With telescopes and long time exposures, astronomers can photograph graceful veils of gas, the remains of matter hurled off by those catastrophically explosive stars called supernovas. The material hurled off contains elements heavier than iron. It now seems that a cloud of such matter from a supernova enriched the gas cloud of hydrogen and helium out of which the Sun and planets of the Solar System formed. The supernova matter shown here is located in the constellation Cygnus the Swan.

The pressure in the core is now so great that the iron is crushed to bits (into neutrons), and the core undergoes a final collapse. In a flash the outer regions of the star also collapse inward and cause a catastrophic explosion called a supernova. During that explosion, which takes only a fraction of a second, the outer layers of gases are hurled away. Energy, including blinding light, is cast off in all directions. So much energy is produced in the star that all the elements heavier than iron—for example, gold, silver, lead, uranium, and others—are produced and also flung outward. When astronomers see this happen to a star, they call it a supernova. Over a few months a new supernova may give off as much light as the Sun produces in a billion years. A supernova visible to the unaided eye burst into view in 1987 in the nearby galaxy called the Large Magellanic Cloud.

At this stage of a supernova explosion there is an immense cloud made up mostly of hydrogen but also containing many billions of tons of all the heavy elements as well. The cloud expands across space at a speed of about 1,000 miles a second. For the moment let's leave that very special cloud containing heavy elements, rushing through space in the direction of a distant star-cloud just beginning to form a new star.

BIRTH OF THE SOLAR SYSTEM
Among the billions of star-clouds made up of hydrogen and helium was one to be called the Sun. Its original gas cloud of hydrogen and helium—lacking any of the heavier elements—spread out some 20 billion miles across space. The cloud contained about twice as much matter as the Sun has today. At some stage the makeup of that cloud was changed in an important way. The gale of heavy elements speeding across space from a supernova explosion met that cloud and enriched its hydrogen and helium with an abundance of heavy elements. So we now have our original Sun cloud, or solar nebula.

As matter from the solar nebula began tumbling in toward the denser central region, the nebula began to spin and flatten. This produced a disk of matter that revolved around a dense central sphere that was contracting into a new Sun, or protosun. As that new star began to heat up and glow a dull red, matter out in the disk started clumping into solid objects. The more massive clumps swept up less massive ones and so grew larger. Some of the clumps were composed of ice, others of rocky matter, and still others contained large amounts of heavier matter, including iron, for example. Some of that ice is preserved to this day as comets and the matter making up Saturn's rings.

The young Sun continued to grow more massive as it gradually drew large amounts of nearby disk matter into itself. But farther out in the disk, as far out as the present distance of Jupiter from the Sun, the Sun's gravitational attraction was less effective. This resulted in the outer regions of the disk having relatively more matter than the inner regions and could explain why the inner planets (Mercury, Venus, Earth, and Mars) are smaller than the outer gas-giant planets (Jupiter, Saturn, Uranus, and Neptune).

Unlike the less massive inner planets, the more massive outer planets were able to attract and hold on to relatively large amounts of gases, which would have included hydrogen, methane, and ammonia, for example. Those three gases make up the bulk of the outer planets' atmospheres today.

In that wide belt of space between Mars and Jupiter are thousands upon thousands of tumbling chunks of rock and metal called the asteroids. Ceres, the largest, is a moonlike globe about 620 miles across. Others are pear shaped or odd-shaped lumps of rock that have been shattered as the asteroids keep smashing into one another.

Where did the asteroids come from—dumbbell-shaped Hektor; pale Eros that tumbles along end-over-end; and dark, ball-shaped Pallas marked with craters? Years ago astronomers suspected that a planet about the size of Mars once orbited the Sun in the middle of what is now the asteroid belt. Is it possible, they wondered, that Jupiter's powerful gravity gradually pulled the planet closer and closer? If so, eventually the planet would have been pulled close enough to Jupiter to be shattered to bits.

One thing that made this idea attractive was that some of the asteroids are all metal, others part metal and part rock, and still others all rock. A shattered planet with a metal core would leave just such a collection of rubble: chunks of metal from the planet's core, part-metal and part-rock pieces from the planet's middle region, and lumps of rock from the crust.

As attractive as this idea was, however, it has been given up. Most astronomers now think that the asteroids are bits and pieces of matter—called planetesimals—left over from the time the planets were formed. Jupiter's powerful gravity most likely kept a planet from forming nearby, and so the asteroids came to be.

EARTH'S VIOLENT YOUTH

As the sweep-up process of solid matter in the solar disk continued, massive clumps began to join and form planet Earth and the other planets. The main ingredients of the dust cloud out of which Earth was formed were hydrogen, helium, carbon, nitrogen, oxygen, iron, aluminum, gold, uranium, sulfur, phosphorus, and silicon. As proto-Earth grew more massive through the sweep-up process, called accretion, the densely packed matter in the core region was under such great pressure that core temperature rose sharply. But there was another source of heat as well—the radioactivity of the elements uranium, thorium, and potassium. More than 4 billion years ago Earth probably was a soupy globe of molten rock and metal at a temperature of some 2,000°C (3,630°F).

Because these molten rock and metal materials were free to flow about, the heavier matter such as iron and nickel sank into the central regions of young Earth where they formed a heavy core. Lighter matter, including silicates, floated up toward the surface. Through this separation process Earth developed an outer layer of lightweight rocky matter made up of silicates and a core of iron and nickel.

As the crust cooled, mountain-size planetesimals continued to smash into Earth, scarring its surface with deep craters like those visible today on Mercury, Mars, and the Moon. Planetesimal bombardments seem very likely to have happened, since large amounts of iron and other metals are found mixed in with Earth's crustal rock. Because the crust was no longer molten when these late-arrival planetesimals, containing large amounts of heavy metals, struck the surface, the metals remained part of Earth's crust instead of sinking into the core region.

Planetesimal bombardment of the inner planets seems to have been common during the first 600 million years, then lessened rapidly between 4.0 and 3.3 billion years ago and has remained rare ever since.

During Earth's molten and then early cooling stages, many gases bubbled out of solution and collected above the new planet as a primitive atmosphere. Among such gases were large amounts of hydrogen, water vapor, nitrogen, carbon monoxide, and carbon dioxide, along with smaller amounts of methane, ammonia, and hydrogen sulfide. The air also was thick with poisonous cyanide and formaldehyde. At this stage there was little or no oxygen, which today makes up 21 percent of our air. The water released from the crustal rocks shot into the air as countless geysers. But it was so hot that the fountains of water simply evaporated into water vapor, which hung in the air.

As more and more water vapor collected in the primitive atmosphere, the environment eventually cooled enough for the vapor to condense out and fall as rain. In some areas, where the surface rock was cool enough, the rain soaked into the dry rock. In other areas, where the rock was still very hot, the rains evaporated back into water vapor and were driven skyward by the heat of the surface. At this stage there was no life of any kind on Earth.

As the crustal rock continued to cool, torrential rains fell day and night for perhaps 100,000 years and collected in pools that in time formed shallow, warm seas. By about 3.9 billion years ago a thin solid crust of rock floated uneasily on a vast sea of molten rock beneath. Sometimes this thin crust was punctured by eruptions from below and molten rock welled up, evaporating some seas and melting huge areas of solid crust. Other times the thin crustal rock was struck and ruptured from above by mountain-size planetesimals still flying around. Planetesimals, meteoroids, and other debris from space burned down through the atmosphere and plummeted to Earth, exploding into vast clouds of dark carbon dust mixed with sulfur fumes. Fiery volcanic plumes and continual lightning brightened the night sky, as did the reddish glow of mammoth lava flows that poured out of openings in the crust.

Meanwhile, ultraviolet energy from the Sun broke down some of the complex gases of the air. It changed ammonia into free hydrogen and nitrogen; methane into carbon and hydrogen; and water vapor into hydrogen and oxygen. The free hydrogen was so light that most of it escaped Earth's gravitational grip. Many such reactions must have taken place in that early atmosphere.

So, if Earth scientists are correct, some 400 million years after our planet had developed a cool and generally stable crust, it accumulated shallow seas and had a new atmosphere of carbon dioxide, carbon monoxide, water vapor, nitrogen, neon, and argon. Gone were the ammonia and methane of former times.

At this stage, some 3.9 billion years ago, Earth was spinning much more rapidly than it is today, at a rate of one complete rotation every ten hours instead of every twenty-four hours, which gave it a daylight period of five hours followed by five hours of night. The reason is that Earth's satellite, the Moon, had not yet had an opportunity to slow Earth's rotation by tidal friction. The effect, as it occurs today, is that the Moon's gravitational attraction tends to hold our planet's ocean water in place while Earth spins beneath the mass of water. Friction between the water and Earth's rock crust acts as a brake that slows down Earth's spin. Rotational braking could not occur until Earth's oceans were formed.

All the time Earth was going through its fiery beginnings—sometimes called the Big Belch because of the great outbursts of gases trapped beneath the crust—the core of the young Sun kept heating up until its temperature reached 10 million kelvins. At that point it began to shine by fusing hydrogen into helium as we see it shining today. At the time the Sun's nuclear furnace ignited, the Sun gave off huge bursts of energy that swept all through the Solar System. These solar gales gradually cleared away the Solar System's dense fog of gas and dust grains through which the newly formed planets had been moving. With the expulsion of this cosmic fog, space between the planets became clear, as it is today.

Although no one can say for certain that the Sun and its family of planets formed just this way, all the evidence points to some such process. In any case, it is almost certain that planets are by-products of star formation and that the stars themselves are born out of vast clouds of mostly hydrogen gas often enriched with atoms of heavy elements forged by the explosion of supernova stars. Our home planet's history spans only the most recent one-third of cosmic history since the Big Bang.

Where the telescope ends, the microscope begins.
Which of the two has the grander view?
—Victor Hugo, 1800s

3

Chemical Evolution and Early Life

AN AGE FOR EARTH

Scientists who study our home planet's early geology and the origin and evolution of life on Earth need to know when certain events in Earth's history happened. That means they need to be able to measure the age of Earth rocks and Moon rocks and to date fossils.

As you found in the previous chapter, evidence favors the idea that the Sun and planets originated at about the same time out of the solar nebula, a cosmic soup of mostly hydrogen mixed with heavy elements cast off by a supernova explosion. Astronomers can make an estimate of when that event took place by studying the Sun. Based on the kind of star the Sun is, they can estimate the amount of hydrogen fuel the Sun has had available to keep shining the way we see it shining today. They also can estimate how rapidly the Sun is using up its fuel. Dividing the rate of fuel used into the amount of fuel available shows that the Sun has a lifespan of about 10 billion years. But the Sun's lifespan is not its age. By "age" we mean the length of time the Sun has been just about as we see it now, the length of time the Sun has been pouring out energy at its present rate. That length of time is estimated at about 5 billion years.

Although we cannot reach out and tear a chunk from the Sun to find out how old its material is, we can reach out and examine pieces of Earth rock, Moon rock, Mars rock, and cosmic debris from the asteroid belt that rains down on Earth as meteorites, in order to measure their ages. Geologists have used various radioactive elements to measure the age of rock samples from every corner of Earth. The oldest rocks yet found are zircon crystals from near Perth, Australia, that are 4.3 billion years old. Rocks from Greenland have been dated at 3.8 billion years. Rocks from other regions—near the Great Lakes and in certain regions of Europe—are 3.5 billion years old.

But this does not mean that Earth was formed only 4.3 billion years ago. That age is for rock that went through its most recent geological change at that time. Earth's various rocks are continually changing as they are worn down by rain, wind, and other agents and turned into sediments such as sand and clay, which are then carried to the sea by streams and rivers. Millions of years later these sediments are crushed and thrust up as mountains of re-formed rock such as the Rockies, which in turn are worn down into sediments again. While Earth has a recorded geologic history going back at least 4.3 billion years, its prehistory, or history before that time, is unknown to us by direct measurement.

The oldest Moon rocks that have yet been examined have a geological history going back nearly a billion years earlier than the oldest Earth rocks. That means that the much smaller Moon had cooled and developed a solid crust earlier than Earth did and that the Moon's surface has changed little to this day.

Meteorites now seem to be the senior citizens of the Solar System. Radioactive dating of many stone and iron meteorites shows an average age of about 4.7 billion years, a figure that agrees nicely with the astronomers' estimate of a 5-billion-year-age for the Sun.

Scientists the world over, using several different methods of dating, agree on a figure of about 4.6 billion years for Earth's age. The figure is well established and as close to a "fact" as science can get.

Generally, different kinds of radioactive elements break down, or decay, at different rates. For instance, because of their slow rate of decay, uranium and thorium "atomic clocks" can be used to date very old rocks; medium-aged rocks are dated by the potassium atomic clock; and younger and once-living matter is dated by the carbon atomic clock. Only rock that was once molten and has cooled—called igneous rock—can be dated by atomic clocks. Such igneous rock includes granite and lava.

Sedimentary rock—solidified sand, clay, limestone, and mud—cannot be dated by direct measurement. Such sedimentary rock includes shale and sandstone, for example. Sometimes, however, when a deposit of sediment is hardening into rock, nearby molten rock may melt its way into the hardening sediment. In this way a sandwich filling of molten rock may be squeezed between two layers of sedimentary rock. When that mixed rock mass cools centuries later, the age of the igneous rock filling can be measured by an atomic clock. If it turns out to be 350 million years old, for example, the neighboring layers of sedimentary rock must also be 350 million years old. A real-life example of such a case is the famous Palisades rock cliffs along the New Jersey side of the Hudson River across from New York City. Since those rocks have been dated at 200 million years old, any fossils preserved in them must also be 200 million years old.

ORIGIN OF LIFE: EARLY IDEAS

Almost every culture that has been studied has creation myths that attempt to explain how life arose. In all such myths a supernatural being, a god of some sort, creates life out of nothing, or out of mud or some other nonliving earthly substance. Since creation myths can neither be proved nor disproved, they are beyond the testing of science. Science deals with the natural world, with things that can be weighed and measured; it cannot deal with the supernatural, which is without substance and cannot be measured.

The idea of life arising out of nonliving matter is thousands of years old. It used to be popularly believed that flies and certain other creatures could arise fully formed out of dust and mud, or out of decaying meat or the flesh of dead fish. Nearly always such a belief in this process, called spontaneous generation, is the result of drawing incorrect conclusions from what seems to be happening.

It wasn't until the mid-1600s that physicians began to test the idea of spontaneous generation and challenge it. One such experimenter was the Italian Francesco Redi. He did experiments showing that maggots, which are the larval stage of flies, are not generated spontaneously by rotting meat. The idea for his experiments came from something he had observed.

Redi had put three dead snakes in a box and from time to time examined them as they were decaying. Soon he noticed that maggots were crawling over the decaying meat and eating it. After a while there was nothing left of the snakes except their bones. Nineteen days after he had put the dead snakes in the box, many of the maggots became inactive and formed themselves into hard balls, what we now know to be the pupal stage in the life cycle of a fly. At the time, however, the idea of life cycles of insects was poorly understood, although Redi was aware that caterpillars go through a pupal stage when they spin a cocoon. The idea of an animal changing its form was difficult to accept.

Redi next put some of the maggot pupae into a jar to find out what would happen. About a week later each pupa broke open and out came an adult fly. Could it be, Redi asked, that the maggots are not created out of dead meat but hatch from tiny eggs laid on the meat by adult flies? It was a hypothesis, an educated guess, and he lost no time testing it.

He put a dead snake in one jar, a dead eel in another, dead flesh from a calf in a third, and some fish flesh in a fourth. Then he did exactly the same with four other identical jars. While he left the first set of jars open to the air, he tightly capped the second set. As he examined both sets each day, he noticed that flies were entering and leaving the open jars, and within a few days he also noticed that maggots were crawling over the meat in all four of the open jars. There wasn't a single maggot on any of the meat in the four closed jars.

Redi, and others, performed more experiments that seemed to seal the fate of spontaneous generation. It seemed certain that living things could be produced only by other living things. Biogenesis, the idea that life arises only from living things and not from nonliving matter, became one of the foundation stones of biology.

But old ideas die hard, and spontaneous generation was not yet finished. One of the culprits was the newly invented microscope, which revealed a whole new world of tiny organisms that could not be seen by the unaided eye. A major question was "How do *these* tiny creatures originate?" Where did the hundreds of different kinds come from? Were they subject to the law of biogenesis, or, since they were so simple, could they be generated from nonliving matter? The whole argument of spontaneous generation was opened up again, since it was impossible to observe any eggs or seeds from which these elusive microscopic organisms developed. If a few strands of hay were placed in pure water, a few days later the water was swarming with the creatures.

Around 1700 Louis Jablot designed an experiment similar to those of Redi. He put some hay into a container of water and then boiled it to kill any living matter that it might contain. Then he poured half the boiled material into a second container and tightly sealed it. After a few days he examined the contents of both containers. While he couldn't find a single living thing in the material from the sealed container, the material from the container that had been left open swarmed with life. He concluded that any material that has been sterilized cannot possibly generate life. The living organisms in the container that had been left open, he said, drifted in from the air.

Still, stubborn believers in spontaneous generation argued that, of course, if you kept air from a purified (boiled) substance, life could not be generated. The reason, they explained, was that air contained a "special life-giving substance" that could not reach the material in the sealed jar.

Around 1800 the French Academy of Science offered a prize to anyone who could settle the spontaneous generation argument. The famous French scientist Louis Pasteur was the one to do it. He argued that the air contained a special life-giving substance, but not a magical one, not a supernatural one. It also contained microorganisms—germs, microbes, bugs, bacteria, or whatever anyone chose to call them. Pasteur showed that two things were true: first, that germs from the air entering milk, wine, water, or meat broth are killed by a specific boiling time; second, that on exposure to the air all such substances become infected with bacteria.

In a wonderfully simple experiment, Pasteur made a glass flask with a long curved neck that narrowed to a small opening (about the size of a pinhole). Milk, beef broth, or any other purified (boiled) substance put in these narrow-neck flasks remained purified even though air could enter the flask through the small opening. What happened was that when bacteria in the air drifted in through the tiny opening, they got trapped in the curved neck and stuck there. He showed that this was so by tilting the flask until some of the liquid ran down and sloshed around where the bacteria were trapped and was then allowed to run back into the main part of the flask. The bacteria also washed back and soon multiplied into a thriving colony.

ORIGIN OF LIFE: CHEMICAL EVOLUTION

We will now return to where we left Earth after it had cooled enough to form a solid rock crust. It had numerous warm shallow seas and an atmosphere of carbon dioxide, carbon monoxide, water vapor, nitrogen, neon, and argon, among other substances. The time was about 4 billion years ago. The continents that we know today had not yet formed and were not to appear for hundreds of millions of years. There were no majestic mountain ranges such as the Rockies or Alps, although there were many volcanic peaks that had built up during the planet's recent and fiery youth. And the length of a day was only about 10 hours long.

At this time in Earth's geologic history an oxygen-rich atmosphere had not yet formed. This meant that the planet lacked that upper-level layer of heavy oxygen called the ozone layer. The ordinary oxygen that we breathe comes in molecules made up of two oxygen atoms each, written in chemical shorthand as O_2. Ozone molecules have three atoms each, O_3. Today the ozone layer screens out most of the Sun's harmful ultraviolet energy, the rays that give you severe sunburn if you lie on the beach too long. If the ozone layer were destroyed, much of life on Earth would be burned to a crisp. But 4 billion years ago there was no ozone screen, which meant a rich source of ultraviolet energy to help mix the chemical soup of those early shallow seas by producing many chemical reactions. Lightning was another source of energy, driving chemical reactions that combined certain atoms as molecules and linked simple molecules to form complex molecules.

In the early 1950s, a graduate student named Stanley Miller, working at the University of Chicago, designed an experiment to find out just what kinds of molecules might have been built before life arose on Earth. Through a closed system of glass tubing Miller circulated a mixture of hydrogen, methane, ammonia, and water vapor and then bombarded the gases with lightning discharges for a week. The water vapor condensed as "rain," and the other gases dissolved in the water. When Miller drew off some of the solution and examined it, he found that a number of complex molecules had been formed, molecules that are needed by all living things. Among them were amino acids, which are the building blocks of proteins. Since then other researchers have repeated Miller's experiment and have produced all sorts of interesting molecules. In fact, they have produced all of the simple building blocks of the complex molecules of living cells, including molecules that build the various cell parts and the energy-rich molecules that drive the many chemical reactions that keep a cell healthy.

The amino acids, proteinlike substances, and other complex molecules that were formed naturally in Earth's early atmosphere on its warm rocks and in its shallow seas were a far cry from living matter. But over a few hundred million years those molecules followed courses of chemical evolution that brought them ever closer to becoming living matter.

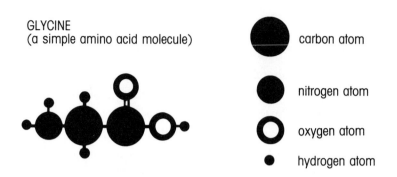

GLYCINE
(a simple amino acid molecule)

● carbon atom

● nitrogen atom

○ oxygen atom

• hydrogen atom

Amino acids are the building blocks of proteins, which our bodies use as food and building matter. There are about twenty different amino acids, of which glycine is a simple one.

The next stage in chemical evolution might have been the grouping of certain complex molecules within a protective bubble membrane. Those molecules would have included amino acids, simple sugars, and molecules containing phosphate. The membrane could have been made of atoms of hydrogen, carbon, phosphorus, and oxygen arranged in such a way that the highly organized and stable molecules within were separated from the disorganized molecules of the outside world. But because the membrane had small openings, there could be a two-way exchange of certain materials between the inside and outside of this nonliving cell. Energy and "food" molecules taken into the cell would have represented a kind of "growth."

According to the biologist Lynn Margulis, these first bubble membranes might have stretched enough to break in two, each half reenclosing and protecting its cargo of organized molecules. Later, she says, molecules within these bubble membranes may have begun to maintain the membranes. These nonliving cells might have remained active until they used up the energy and building supply molecules available to them. After that, their activity would have stopped.

The next step was for "smarter" protocells, as we can call these nonliving cells, to make their own food rather than depend on an outside source of ready-made food. We can imagine these advanced protocells taking in from the outside environment very simple nutrient molecules and combining them once inside into usable "food." Simple raw-material nutrient molecules would have been in greater supply than the more complex ready-made ones. Such advanced protocells would have had an obvious edge over their simpler competitors. Examples of such organisms today are the many different kinds of green plants that take in the raw materials carbon dioxide and water vapor from the air and fashion them into their own complex food, glucose, a sugar.

During this period of some 200 million years of chemical evolution, protocells acquired another important feature—that of making other protocells exactly like themselves. The key to this ability was a complex giant molecule called RNA (ribonucleic acid) that became a part of protocells. RNA formed in those countless small shallow seas and became enclosed within bubble membranes. RNA had the ability to select from the chemical environment certain amino acids and other chemical building blocks (nucleotides) and assemble them into protein molecules. Those protein molecules could then start the process of making more RNA. In this way RNA could assemble amino acids into proteins and produce more giant molecules exactly like itself. So at one stage RNA and proteins were the two chief features of protocells. The RNA was the control center, while the protein molecules served as food and building materials.

During this same period, but probably after the formation of RNA, another important giant molecule evolved—DNA (deoxyribonucleic acid). If we think of RNA as a "doer," we can think of DNA as the master "planner." DNA carries the instructions that tell RNA what kind of protein to make. Every living cell of every known organism on Earth has both DNA and RNA. And the particular kind of protein that DNA instructs RNA to make determines that you are you and not an eagle or an elm tree.

All organisms ever studied are made of protein molecules assembled from only about twenty different amino acids. The amino acids are joined as chains of a few to several hundred amino acid links. And those vital links—the very common denominator of all living things—are not only made by your body but can also be made in a test tube and have been found in meteorites.

THE FIRST LIVING CELLS

The commonness of DNA and protein linking all life on Earth is our best evidence that the ancestors of life can be traced back nearly 4 billion years. Sometime between 3.5 billion and 4 billion years ago, membranes enclosing some watery fluid, a collection of protein molecules, RNA, and DNA evolved as the first living cells—organisms that today we call bacteria and that are found by the trillions virtually everywhere. They drift about in the air ready to infect us with disease; they live in the soil and make it fertile; they live in the lake-bottom ooze without oxygen; and they live on and in our bodies where they help digest our food, rid us of wastes, and manufacture vitamin K for our use. Your body is home for some 100 quadrillion (100,000,000,000,000,000) bacterial cells.

The ability of bacteria to reproduce is astounding. Each bacterium simply divides in two, in a process biologists call binary fission, or simple division. Where there was one bacterium, 20 minutes later the one has divided in two, producing a second bacterium identical to itself. The

Bacteria multiply at an astonishing rate by binary fission. Before dividing into two new bacteria, the "parent" bacterium enlarges and duplicates its DNA. The now double organism next pinches itself in two. The process takes about 20 minutes. If you start off with a single bacterium and binary fission goes on for 48 hours, how many bacteria will there be at the end of that time?

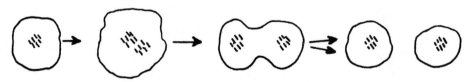

BINARY FISSION

two are identical because they have the same kind of DNA and RNA. The two then divide to produce four, and so on. In just one day a single bacterium can give rise to a million others like itself! Bacteria come in three different shapes, depending on their way of life. Some are ball shaped, others are shaped like short rods, and others look like bundles of spiral noodles. Many of those built on a spiral body plan are parasites; their corkscrew motion enables them to drill through the skin or lining of the digestive system and into the moist tissues of their hosts.

We have fossil evidence that bacterial cells were around 3.5 billion years ago. Once established, those inventive sacs of DNA, RNA, and protein reproduced at an astonishing rate. They were without enemies and had a limitless supply of energy and food. So the evolution of living matter unmistakably began at least 3.5 billion years ago.

Complex organisms are composed of cells, which are composed
of molecules, which are composed of atoms; and it is not clear
at what level of complexity life first emerges.

—Alexander Koyre, 1965

4

The First Billion
and a Half Years

THE AGE OF BACTERIA

Once established in the many small, warm ponds dotting Earth's surface
some 3.5 billion years ago, the first bacterial cells spread explosively.
They took up life on the land, some being carried far and wide on the
winds of an oxygenless air. The Age of Bacteria was in full swing. Broad
blankets of bacteria stretching from horizon to horizon transformed the
landscape.

Biologist Lynn Margulis and her coauthor Dorion Sagan in their
book *Microcosmos,* imagine a scene of

> . . . brilliantly colored pools abounding and mysterious greenish
> and brownish patches of scum floating on the waters, stuck to the
> banks of rivers, tinting the damp soils like fine molds. A ruddy
> sheen would coat the stench-filled waters. Shrunk to microscopic
> perspective, a fantastic landscape of bobbing purple, aquamarine,
> red, and yellow spheres would come into view. Inside the violet
> spheres of *Thiocapsa,* suspended yellow globules of sulfur would emit

bubbles of skunky gas. Colonies of ensheathed viscous organisms would stretch to the horizon. One end stuck to rocks, the other ends of some bacteria would insinuate themselves inside tiny cracks and begin to penetrate the rock itself. Long skinny filaments would leave the pack of their brethren, gliding by slowly, searching for a better place in the sun. Squiggling bacterial whips shaped like corkscrews of fusili pasta would dart by. Multicellular filaments and tacky, textilelike crowds of bacterial cells would wave with the currents, coating pebbles with brilliant shades of red, pink, yellow, and green. Showers of spores, blown by breezes, would splash and crash against the vast frontier of low-lying muds and waters.

That probably was the scene some 2.5 billion years ago, after a billion years of bacterial evolution. By that time there were many different kinds of bacteria, one group differing from others in its ability to thrive amid especially high temperatures, for example, or another group needing lots of sunlight as opposed to those that got on nicely with relatively little light, or still other groups having adapted to large or small amounts of salts in the water. All such adaptations to different conditions in the environment led to diversity among populations.

As Earth became increasingly populated by bacteria, their chemical interaction with their surroundings was bound to change the environment in many ways. For example, the waste gases given off by a large group of bacteria might have accumulated in amounts that became poisonous. Those bacteria unable to cope with such environmental threats would die, while those able to cope would be selected by nature for survival, a process called natural selection.

Of every million divisions among a group of bacteria, one new bacterium will have DNA different from that of its parent. The DNA may become different because part of its molecule was bombarded by radiation, or because it was rearranged slightly by contact with a harmful chemical. Such bacteria, or any other organism with altered DNA, is called a mutant. And the changed DNA is called a mutation.

Nearly all mutations are harmful and the mutant usually dies. It

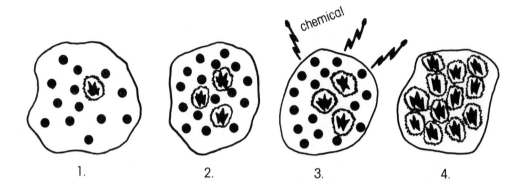

How environmental change may reshape a population: Suppose a population of organisms acquires a mutant individual (1) that survives and reproduces more of its kind that also survive (2). Then the environment is changed by the introduction of a chemical (3) that gradually kills all organisms in the population except those carrying the mutation (4). The new and surviving population of mutants now all have DNA that makes the population adapted to the changed environment.

dies because the changed DNA affects the ability of the mutant to get on in its environment. But occasionally a mutation is beneficial and allows the bacterium, or other organism, to survive amid environmental change—in unusually high temperatures or unusually low temperatures, for example. Such a successful mutant among bacteria thrives in a condition that might be harmful to other bacteria in the population, and it quickly gives rise to an entirely new population with DNA just like its own.

Among other environmental crises that bacteria had to face and overcome from time to time were drought or flood, or changes in the air quality brought on by volcanoes that vented vast clouds of dust and noxious gases. Where successful mutations abounded, new populations quickly arose fully adapted to a new environmental condition that spelled doom to populations not adapted.

Differences in DNA among individuals in any population are called variations. And mutations among all living things are the "raw materials" of variation.

At least 3 billion years ago, sex among bacteria was invented, not sex as we think of it in the popular way, but the exchange of DNA between bacteria. That is what biologists mean by "sex": the exchange of DNA between individuals. Bacteria were able to exchange DNA in a number of ways: For example, they took in DNA left by a dead cell and added parts of it to their own DNA; or they became "infected" with foreign DNA carried by a virus; or two bacteria joined temporarily side by side and exchanged DNA. To this day bacteria continue to have several opportunities to exchange DNA. Among the early bacteria, evolution took a giant step forward when sections of DNA between two individuals got exchanged and mixed as a matter of course.

In its simplest form, then, evolution is change in those sections of DNA called genes. We can think of genes as units of inheritance that gave you blond or black hair, brown or blue eyes, and so on. Genetic change gives rise to a new type of individual who can pass on a beneficial mutation to its offspring. It is the ease with which bacteria are able to exchange genes, or DNA, that caused such wide diversity among them beginning 3.5 billion years ago.

So far in our account of ceaseless chemical activity that led to the making of the first living cells—bacteria—we have not mentioned the chief thing that sets bacteria apart from all other life. We tend to think of life on Earth as either plants or animals. Although a useful scheme in some ways, it is not very helpful at this stage in our story of evolution because neither plants nor animals had evolved. Bacteria were the only living things and were to be the only living things for 2 billion years. Bacteria do not qualify for status as either plants or animals. Biologists put them in a separate group, or kingdom, apart from the plant kingdom and animal kingdom.

What makes bacteria different from all other living things is their small size and the way every bacterial cell is organized, or the way it *isn't* organized. If we took a bacterial cell apart, first we would break through the soft membrane that holds the cell together and that lets nutrient molecules in and waste molecules out. Beneath the membrane we would find a sea of watery matter called cytoplasm, which all living cells have. Drifting about in the cytoplasmic sea is a single molecule of DNA along with some RNA. There are also several knobby structures called ribosomes and some molecules that store energy in the form of a substance called ATP. The DNA tells the RNA what kind of protein to make. The RNA then attaches to a ribosome where it makes protein, and the ATP supplies the energy to make it all happen.

In all of nature that we know about, there are two major groups of cells. Bacterial cells form one of the groups, called prokaryotes. Prokaryotes were to rule supreme as the only kind of cell for 2 billion years.

In a moment we will describe a new kind of cell, larger and much more organized than the prokaryotes, that came along, but not before recounting a world-wide event brought about by certain of the bacteria-prokaryotes. It was the greatest natural "catastrophe" that Earth has ever experienced. It was the introduction into the environment of huge amounts of a gas that was poisonous to nearly all cells living at the time—oxygen.

THE OXYGEN REVOLUTION

While most bacteria still grazed on ready-made food molecules, certain others evolved the ability to make their own food out of free hydrogen and carbon dioxide in the air. These were the cyanobacteria, bacteria that thrive in bright sunlight and exist to this day virtually unchanged after more than 3 billion years. The energy of sunlight provides the energy needed for those bacteria to combine hydrogen with carbon dioxide to produce food—sugars. In the process, oxygen is given off to the air as waste. This important ability to make complex (sugar) molecules out of the simple hydrogen and carbon dioxide molecules is called photosynthesis. Today photosynthesis is carried out by all green plants and is Earth's supplier of oxygen.

But more than 2 billion years ago, even though the cyanobacteria had been carrying out photosynthesis for some time, Earth's atmosphere contained hardly any oxygen. As quickly as oxygen was released, it was gobbled up by oxygen-hungry molecules, including sulfur, carbon, and hydrogen. So for millions of years there had been very little, if any, build-up of free oxygen in the air.

Until this time in our story, there had been lots of hydrogen in the atmosphere, but the supply was gradually running out. Energy pouring out of the Sun had been sweeping much of the hydrogen away. And Earth's gravitational grip was not strong enough to keep the ever-dwindling supply of lightweight atoms and molecules of hydrogen as part of its air. The cyanobacteria also had been helping drain the supply. But eventually these hydrogen-hungry bacteria evolved a way to get hydrogen from water.

With this new and near-limitless supply of hydrogen, the cyano-bacteria spread far and wide, displacing populations of other bacteria that could not make their own food through photosynthesis. Rapidly, many areas of Earth were turned a blue green tint, the color of the cyanobacteria themselves that spread along riverbanks, formed a scum on ponds, and covered mud flats.

All the while the blue-greening of Earth continued, oxygen produced by the cyanobacteria was pouring into the air and being absorbed ever more slowly. Then came a time when oxygen began to build up and was there to stay. And that was when the trouble started. Unless an organism is properly packaged so that it is protected from oxygen, it will be poisoned. Given a chance, free oxygen quickly combines with and breaks down the complex molecules of living matter. It combines with and breaks down DNA, RNA, and vitamins. It destroys proteins and breaks up cell membranes, killing a cell instantly.

The bacteria that were releasing all this free oxygen into the air were in as much danger of being destroyed as were all other bacteria exposed to free oxygen. Many populations were wiped out immediately. Natural selection favored those populations that had adpated to life zones in mud flats, swamp bottoms, and other places where free oxygen could not reach. Such bacteria, unchanged through the ages, exist today.

Whenever any major change occurs in the environment, there are organisms waiting and able to thrive amid the change. Their ability to do so is explained in the one word—*mutation.* Among the populations not doomed by the oxygen revolution were mutants that were not affected by oxygen and that produced it through photosynthesis. Those mutant strains of bacteria multiplied, and their new populations took over, their success in the new environment assured. In fact, the cyanobacteria that had started the oxygen revolution came to depend on oxygen for survival.

Oxygen respiration was a new and greatly improved way of living. Oxygen quickly broke down the large food molecules of sugar so that they could be used as energy and converted into protein. Oxygen respiration produced eighteen times more energy than the old way of life could. So the cyanobacteria produced oxygen by photosynthesis and used it for nourishment and waste management through respiration. Mutations among bacteria other than the blue-greens also evolved new strains that came to depend on oxygen.

By this time the air probably contained very nearly today's percentage of oxygen (21 percent). But exactly when this occurred is hotly argued among scientists. Margulis and others think that 2 billion years ago the air contained about half the amount of oxygen that it has today, and that by 600 million years ago there was nearly as much oxygen as we now have. Evidence in favor of a 2-billion-year-old age for atmospheric oxygen are sediments of that age containing iron that had been changed to rust by oxygen.

It seems likely that planet-wide oxygen levels are maintained, at least in part, by green plants and some bacteria that produce the gas and animals and other bacteria that use it. If the oxygen level were to be lowered by only a few percent, most life on Earth would die from oxygen starvation. And, in theory, if it were to increase by only a few percent, the world's forests would explode into fire and most life would burn up by spontaneous combustion.

By the time the oxygen level in the air had reached 21 percent, the energy of sunlight had caused some of the oxygen atoms to join and form that layer of heavy oxygen we call ozone. The ozone layer immediately became a shield that blocked out high-energy ultraviolet rays. This caused still another important change in the chemistry taking place at the surface. Without this source of high energy, the production of amino acids and other large molecules needed for life, which had been going on by itself for more than 2 billion years, stopped. But by this time most of the prokaryotes had come to make their own complex molecules out of simpler materials.

Life would never be the same again. The stage was set for an explosion of evolutionary activity.

THE RISE OF SUPERCELLS

Sometime during those several hundred million years, as the oxygen level was building up in the atmosphere, a new kind of cell appeared on the scene. The difference between the old bacterial prokaryotes and the new arrivals—called eukaryotes—was as striking as the difference between an old-fashioned cash register and a computer. Two new features set the eukaryotes off from the bacteria.

First, the DNA of these new cells was packaged in a membrane sac located in the center of the cell and separated from the watery cytoplasm just outside. This new control center with its own private environment is called the cell nucleus. When these new cells needed new supplies of protein for growth, the RNA in the nucleus got its instructions from the DNA, slipped through the nuclear membrane and out into the cytoplasm. It then attached to a ribosome and began making protein. Instead of having a single loop of DNA, the new eukaryotes had masses of it in beaded strands coated with protein. The DNA strands in eukaryotic cells are folded back and forth on themselves many times and form those bundles of genes we call chromosomes. If all of the DNA contained in the nucleus of every cell in your body were uncoiled and stretched out into a straight line, it would reach from Earth to the Moon and back more than a million times!

The second new feature of eukaryotes was a cell part called a mitochondrion. The mitochondria had their own membranes, their own DNA, and they captured and used oxygen to provide energy for all of a cell's inner workings.

Some of the newcomer eukaryotes had still another cell part, called a plastid. Plastids are what enabled certain of the prokaryotes to carry out photosynthesis and so make their own food. Those eukaryotes that contained plastids, in addition to mitochondria, also could carry out photosynthesis and make their own food.

We can think of the plastid-containing eukaryotes as early plantlike cells; and we can think of those eukaryotes lacking plastids as early animallike cells. In a sense, then, animals evolved before plants. Since

There are two major divisions of cells: (1) prokaryotes, or bacterial cells, which have in the place of a nucleus a single molecule of DNA and some RNA, as well as ribosomes, cytoplasm, a cell membrane, and an outer cell wall; and (2) eukaryotes, which include all plant and animal cells. Plant cells, unlike animal cells, have a tough cell wall and are box-shaped. All green plant cells also contain plastids, which enable the plant to carry out photosynthesis.

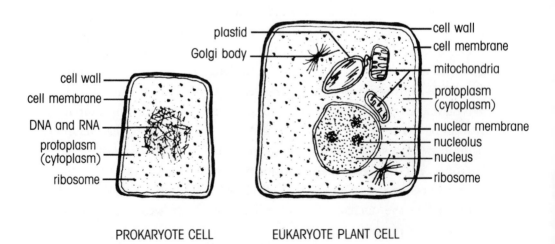

PROKARYOTE CELL   EUKARYOTE PLANT CELL

the eukaryotes with plastids could make their own food, they had no need to live on a diet of other eukaryotes or bacteria. But the eukaryotes lacking plastids had no choice but to lead a predator's life and gobble up anyone they could.

Where did the eukaryotes come from? Margulis thinks that when the prokaryotes were building up the atmosphere's oxygen supply, mitochondria had evolved as free-living organisms. She further thinks that at one stage mitochondria invaded bacterial cells and so found a new home. While a bacterium provided a mitochondrion with food and a safe place to live, the mitochondrion provided the bacterium with a way to get energy from oxygen and a way to dispose of waste molecules by breaking them down with oxygen. Not a bad exchange.

Margulis thinks that a similar story can be told for plastids—that they, too, were once free-living and probably were regularly taken in and intended as food by certain bacteria. But some of the plastids simply wouldn't be digested. Those plastids then became part of the bacterium and in exchange for shelter gave the bacterium the ability to make its own food through photosynthesis. Again, not a bad exchange, if that's what actually happened.

Plastids are even more like free-living bacteria than are mitochondria. Plastids have their own DNA and RNA, their own ribosomes for the manufacture of protein, they are enclosed within their own membrane, and they divide to produce more plastids. Today every green plant contains plastids. They are the green pigments that trap sunlight and enable green plants to produce oxygen and make sugar, which the entire animal kingdom depends on for food.

When two different organisms join as one, the relationship is called symbiosis, meaning "living together." If each provides a vital function for the other, the relationship is called mutualism. The resulting complex organism is more efficient than either of the individual parts was alone. There are hundreds of examples of mutualism today. Were it not for certain bacteria living in the guts of cows and horses, those animals would not be able to digest grass and hay. While a cow provides food and a safe place to live for the bacteria, the bacteria enable the cow to digest grass and hay. Mutualism has been one of the chief driving forces of evolution.

Eukaryotes seem to have begun to evolve when oxygen was changing the planet, and they appear fully evolved as fossils about 1.5 billion years old. More complex than their prokaryotic ancestors, the new eukaryotes eventually gave rise to all of the plants and animals known to us throughout geologic time.

The first eukaryotes may have been the single-cell amoebas and algae (green pond scum) that abound today. The eukaryotes were much larger than their ancestor prokaryotes, and for a good reason. Among them were some that ate others since they lacked plastids and so could not make their own food. Now the bigger you were as a eukaryote, the less likely you would be gobbled up by a smaller neighbor, and the greater your chances of gobbling up someone else. The cyanobacteria of the seas, once so abundant, seem to have been especially hard hit by the predator eukaryotes, since the cyanobacteria groups began to decline. So at this time evolution, and natural selection, looked kindly on bigness as a means of survival. But that was not always to be so.

Eventually, the fossil record tells us, certain eukaryotic cells began to take up life in groups, or colonies. Perhaps, on dividing, certain of the new cells didn't detach completely from the parent cell, and other such incomplete divisions might have produced stringlike groupings of cells. Such a string colony could then wrap around a pebble and anchor itself for protection against the battering of swirling water. Its large size also could protect it from predators. Natural selection would tend to favor such groupings for survival.

In each string colony every cell behaved exactly like every other cell and did not perform any special tasks. Each cell reproduced and carried out all the functions of every other cell in the colony. If a cell living alone were punctured, it died. But if a cell that was part of a colony were killed, the colony would go on living.

The next step was for evolution to build a better colony. This

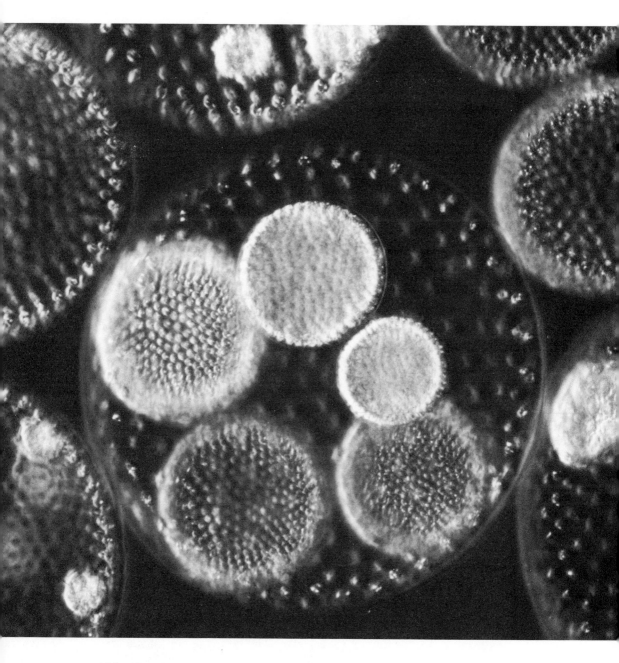

Although Volvox aureus *is usually described as a "colony" of cells, it can be regarded as a simple multicellular organism, since some of its cells are specialized to carry out the function of reproduction.*

happened when certain cells of a colony did certain things that the other cells could not do. The green alga *Volvox* is an example. It is a colony of from hundreds to tens of thousands of cells. Each individual cell has two whiplike threads, called flagella, which can be moved to push the cell around. Each cell also has a plastid, a nucleus, cytoplasm, and a light-sensitive spot that serves as a primitive "eye."

A *Volvox* colony shows both cooperation and specialization. In order for any multicellular, or many-celled, organism to survive, cooperation among its cells must be the rule. For instance, *Volvox* spins as it moves through the water, like a football in flight. If each cell of *Volvox* moved its flagella independently of its neighbors, *Volvox*'s motion would be chaotic, like that of a scull crew where each oarsman rows in a different direction and not in time with the others.

The cells at the surface of *Volvox* are a bit smaller than those nearer the inside. The smaller cells are specialized for using the flagella to move *Volvox* through the water. The larger cells have nothing to do with motion but are specialized to carry out the task of reproduction. Each of these larger cells can produce both large and small cell types.

At this stage in our account of life on Earth, we have moved the geological clock forward about 4 billion years. A small part of that time was taken up with the chemical evolution that led to the many kinds of bacteria that occupied every nook and cranny of Earth's surface and its seas and ponds some 3.5 billion years ago. By far the most of those 4 billion years saw countless millions of experiments in the evolution of those bacteria that must have come in near limitless shapes, colors, and ways of coping with the changing environment.

Then toward the end of those 4 billion years, evolution took off in a grand style and at a dizzying pace. The ancient prokaryotes evolved into the more complex and more efficient eukaryotes, which gave rise to all living things known to us today. The first stage in the eukaryotes' evolutionary wizardry was the building of colonies of cells with specialized tasks. From there it was a short step to the evolution of plants and animals that come close to those we know today.

By some 700 million years ago there were numerous soft-bodied animals living in globelike and wormlike forms in the seas. Because they were soft bodied, their fossils in sandstone show few details of their structure. The oldest fossils of these early animals were found near Sydney, in southeastern Australia. Others similar to them have been found all around the world. It is likely that early relatives of starfish and sea urchins also lived in the seas some 700 million years ago. Many other such soft-bodied animals that only occasionally became fossils must have bridged the time between the early appearance of colonies of cells and the complex plants and animals with hard parts that became such abundant and perfect fossils 200 million years later.

We will now stop the hands of the geological clock at about 600 million years ago. In only a short time after that, geologically speaking, a staggering number of highly complex animals and plants had evolved. Before telling their story, though, we will briefly meet some of the people who first considered the possibility of living things evolving from nonliving matter.

There is grandeur in this view of life, with its several powers, having been originally breathed into a few forms or into one; and that, while this planet has gone cycling on according to the fixed laws of gravity, from so simple a beginning endless forms most beautiful and most wonderful have been, and are being, evolved.

—*Charles Darwin, 1859*

5

Evolution: From Theory to Fact

EARLY IDEAS ABOUT EVOLUTION

That living things evolved from nonliving matter soon after Earth formed is not a new idea, and evolution was not the brain child of the famous English naturalist Charles Darwin, who lived in the first half of the 1800s. However, Darwin did much more to develop a sound theory of evolution, based on years of research, than any other naturalist before his time.

The Greek scholars who lived around the time of Aristotle (384–322 B.C.) did not believe that species evolved along with Earth itself. Like Aristotle, who has been called "the father of natural history," they never imagined that simpler organisms such as single-cell bacteria could change into higher types of organisms such as multicell algae, for example. For them, species were well defined and unchanging. Dogs would be dogs forever. The idea that species do not change in response to major changes in the environment held firm until the 1700s.

The French scientist George-Louis Leclerc, Comte de Buffon, born in 1707, was among the first to propose that species change. He said that changes in the environment brought about physical changes in plants and animals. He also said that those physical changes were passed on from parents to offspring, although at that time no one understood how that could be done. Today we know that the molecule of inheritance, DNA, is the agent.

Buffon further said that life on Earth had existed for millions of years. That idea contradicted what was then believed and taught by Christian fundamentalists whose interpretation of the Bible led them to think that Earth was only a few thousand years old. In 1654 the influential biblical scholar James Ussher, archbishop of Armagh, Ireland, maintained that God had created the universe at 9:00 A.M. on October 26, 4004 B.C. Even today, Christian fundamentalist geologists and biologists who teach at Christian Heritage College in San Diego, California, will tell you that Earth is no more than about ten thousand years old.

Darwin's grandfather, Erasmus Darwin, was another who developed ideas about evolution. He said that millions of years ago there had been a primitive parent organism that had given rise to all the living things about us today. Over those millions of years, he said, the countless offspring of the original parent kept changing, improving by becoming more fit and evolving into more complex forms. In 1794 he wrote: "Would it be too bold to imagine that in the great length of time since the earth began to exist perhaps millions of ages before the history of mankind . . . all warm-blooded animals have arisen from one living filament?"

The French biologist Jean Baptiste de Lamarck was the first to come up with a full-fledged theory of evolution. In 1809, the year Darwin was born, Lamarck proposed that evolution takes place as individual animals and plants acquire new and beneficial characters—in effect, because they try harder! The newly acquired character—a longer reach, a faster gait, a keener nose, a larger or greener leaf—would then be passed on from parent to offspring.

Over a period of three generations, short-antlered deer could evolve into long-antlered animals. At first, all members of the species would have short antlers. Because longer antlers are more useful as a means of protection, individual deer could acquire longer antlers through intensive use, according to Lamarck. Individuals of the next generation would inherit the longer antlers from their parents. In turn, they would increase their antler length and pass on the still greater length to their offspring, and so on until the antlers reached the "most useful" length. Lamarck viewed evolution as a process of "increasing perfection" of individual organisms, but it was an idea that was doomed to fail.

Darwin was just seventeen and a first-year medical student when he heard about Lamarck's views on evolution. Later, Darwin was to recall that he "listened in silent astonishment, and as far as I can judge, without any effect on my mind. I had previously read the [book on evolution written by] my grandfather, in which similar views are maintained, but without producing any effect on me."

At first, this total lack of interest in evolution may seem to be in glaring contradiction to Darwin's most intense interest in later life. We find a clue to Darwin as a scientist and to Darwin's early disinterest in evolution in a comment he made in later life about his grandfather's book: "I was much disappointed [in it], the proportion of speculation being so large to the facts given." Darwin hungered for hard evidence gained through observation, evidence that would either buttress a lofty idea or utterly demolish it. Later, he was to spend nearly 50 years painstakingly gathering mountains of evidence and building his own ideas of evolution through natural selection.

That fact-gathering phase of his life began in 1831 when he signed on as ship's naturalist aboard H.M.S. *Beagle.* The *Beagle* was a 240-ton warship fitted out for surveying. Its mission was to chart the coasts of South America. The ship was under the command of Captain (later, Admiral) FitzRoy, who at age twenty-three was a year older than Darwin.

FitzRoy, a hot-blooded believer in every word of the Bible being true, wanted a naturalist along for two reasons—to examine the coasts for possible valuable mineral deposits, and to find proof that the biblical account of the creation of Earth and all of its life was scientifically true.

Over the next 5 years Darwin was to collect thousands of fossils, send home thousands more descriptions and examples of living plants and animals, and make endless observations of the relationships between living organisms, their behavior, and their environments.

Over those years Darwin could not drive one important thought from his mind: All of the fossils of extinct giant animals he unearthed during the voyage closely resembled living animals he had observed. For example, there was a huge armadillolike animal among his fossils, a giant relative of armadillos living today. And there was an enormous fossil version of today's South American sloths. Darwin marveled over the close relationships between certain extinct species and what he believed to be their modern descendants. He had no doubt that these likenesses between species of the past and the present would "throw more light on the appearance of organic beings on earth and their disappearance from it."

DARWIN'S FINCHES

One of the most important observations Darwin made during the voyage took place at the Galapagos Islands, about 500 miles off the coast of Ecuador. These volcanic islands had boiled up out of the sea floor more than 100 million years ago. During his time ashore Darwin counted twenty-six species of land birds. That in itself was not important, but the fact that twenty-five of those species were unknown elsewhere in the world interested him very much.

Although the idea of natural selection did not strike Darwin with full force until years later, the idea of evolution did come to him at the Galapagos. On each island he was collecting and identifying the different species of birds to be found there. Among them were thirteen species of finches. Darwin kept all of the birds collected on James Island in one

The beak structure of Galapagos finches studied by Darwin ranged from stubby parrotlike beaks, good for cracking nuts, to long thin beaks adapted for prying insects out of bark crevices.

bag, those collected on Chatham Island in another bag, and so on. In this way he could tell just where he had collected each specimen.

As he began to study the finches, he noticed that some were black and others brownish. Despite the differences in color, they all looked rather alike: All had shortish tails and similarly shaped bodies, built the same kinds of nests, and laid the same number and same color eggs. They also generally resembled the finches found on the South American mainland. There was, however, a striking difference among the beaks of the Galapagos finches. They could be arranged, or graded, from a stubby, parrotlike beak at one extreme to a long thin beak at the other extreme.

Those finches with the heavy, parrotlike beaks could crack tough nuts and crush seeds, which adapted them to a certain kind of diet. The finches with long, pointed beaks could not crack nuts; these finches were adapted to a different kind of diet that consisted of soft fruits and flowers. Still others had beaks adapted for catching insects on the wing or for probing into the cracks of bark in search of insects. Darwin marveled over this difference in beak structure among the various finch populations. But he had not yet discovered the most remarkable thing about these birds.

"To my astonishment," he later recalled, "I discovered that all the finches from Charles Island belonged to one species [and had the same shape beak]; all from Albermarle Island belonged to another species [and had the same shape beak]; and all from James and Chatham Islands to still other species."

What did it all mean? Could it be that here on these islands remote "both in space and time we seem to be brought somewhat nearer to that great fact—that mystery of mysteries—the first appearance of new beings on this Earth?"

Darwin imagined a time in the past when the islands of the Galapagos had just risen out of the sea. There was nothing but the cooling black lava. Over many thousands of years, various species of land birds from the mainland found their way to the islands, and seeds from their droppings took hold in the soil that was forming on the rock. Some species survived, others did not.

As plant life continued to spread over each of the islands, the various populations of animals settling there either adapted to the particular environment of a particular island or perished for lack of food. Darwin pictured one species of finch that survived and spread over the islands and must have been the original ancestor of the thirteen species he had collected. Those finch species with beaks adapted for breaking open and crushing nuts evolved on those islands where nuts were plentiful. Those species with beaks adapted for eating fruit evolved on those islands where fruit was plentiful. Those species with beaks adapted for a diet of insects could exist alongside the nut-eaters or the fruit-eaters, since there was no competition for food among the three species. Of the fourteen finch species now living on the islands, three feed on seeds found on the ground, seven feed on insects in different ways, and three feed on cactus in different ways.

The fourteenth species is especially interesting. It feeds on insects lodged in the bark of trees by prying out the insects with a cactus needle as a tool. So natural selection provided this species with a special behavior instead of a special beak structure. This specialized behavior, like the specialized beak structure in the other species, is passed on from parent to offspring by special genes on the species' DNA.

WORKING IT ALL OUT

Darwin returned home on October 2, 1836, and over the next 20 years worked out his theory of evolution through natural selection. He interviewed breeders of pigeons, cattle, dogs, sheep, and goldfish. He experimented with and studied earthworms, bees, moths, butterflies, orchids and other plants. Tirelessly he collected more and more evidence that showed that natural selection is ever at work weeding out the less fit individuals in a population and favoring the more fit, "fitness" meaning how well a population is able to adapt to its environment.

During his interviews with expert breeders of domestic animals and plants, several things were made clear to Darwin. For instance, certain characteristics of an animal could be passed on from parent to offspring. A dairyman selected from his herd of milk cows a few that gave the most milk. He then mated those cows with his prize bull. By selecting out of each new generation of cows those that gave the most milk and then by breeding those cows only, the dairyman would eventually have a herd of cows that gave much more milk than a herd made up of a mixture of good, mediocre, and poor milk cows.

Pigeon breeders, rose breeders, and vegetable growers alike had clearly shown that a species could be made to change (evolve) in dramatic ways by selective breeding. "I soon perceived that selection was the keystone of man's success in making useful races of animals and plants," Darwin wrote. But he was careful to draw a line between "natural" selection as it occurs in nature, and "controlled" selection as it is practiced by animal and plant breeders.

The mail brought to Darwin's study on June 18, 1858, contained a letter from a young naturalist named Alfred Russell Wallace who was studying the plants and animals of the East Indies. When Darwin read the letter, he was shocked. Almost word for word, there was his idea about how new species arise through natural selection. If Darwin saw any merit in Wallace's ideas, Wallace asked, would he please forward the little essay on to the famous geologist and friend of Darwin's, Charles Lyell? But, Wallace went on, if Darwin thought the idea absurd then would he please destroy the essay?

Immediately Darwin sent Lyell the copy of Wallace's essay, warmly praising it. Today both men are credited with developing the principle of evolution through natural selection, although Darwin is credited with developing it first since he had begun writing down his ideas some 20 years earlier.

Darwin imagined the evolution of new species taking extremely long periods of time, many millions of years. While this seems to be true in most cases of the evolution of new species, it is not true in all cases. The fossil record shows many instances of the "sudden" appearance of new species, in some cases involving major changes in body plan, for example. To account for such evolutionary spurts, modern biologists have broadened Darwin's ideas about evolution. In later chapters we will examine this new thinking about evolution.

THE BATTLE OVER EVOLUTION

In November 1859, Darwin's famous book describing evolution through natural selection, *On the Origin of Species by Means of Natural Selection,* was published, and on the first day all 1,250 copies were sold and a new printing was ordered. Darwin sat back in dread, waiting for the outburst he knew would soon follow.

In the early and mid-1800s many scientists and clergymen saw only a blurred dividing line between science and religion. In fact, many scientists were also clergymen and were unyielding in their belief that God had created each and every species and that species could not change. To these people, the idea of evolution through natural selection was a threat to religion, a denial of the existence of God. This was why the religious fundamentalists were so hostile toward the idea of evolution in Darwin's time, and why they continue to be opposed today.

By the spring of 1860 the storm had broken. "Darwinism" was being attacked from pulpits and in classrooms. Blistering reviews of the book were appearing in scientific journals. Darwin was unjustly accused of saying that man was descended from apes and monkeys, an erroneous argument antievolutionists used then and continue to use to this day. People making such attacks either failed to understand Darwin's carefully presented explanation of how evolution works, or they deliberately twisted his ideas in order to discredit him.

The next battleground was the Oxford University meeting in June of the British Association for the Advancement of Science. There was to be a debate on Darwinism, and the word was out to come and watch evolution and the atheist Darwin be "smashed." If the clergy and a handful of scientists had their way, Darwinism would be crushed once and for all. More than seven hundred people attended the debate. Britain's leading botanist, Joseph Hooker, and leading zoologist, T. H. Huxley, were to speak in defense of evolution through natural selection. Bishop Samuel Wilberforce, representing the clergy, was to attack it. It was Wilberforce who had said that he was out to "smash" Darwin, to reveal him as a fraud and evolution as a lie.

So polished and smooth were Wilberforce's sermons that he was popularly known as Soapy Sam. In the debate he spoke first and went straight to the point. Any reputable scientist, he declared, knows perfectly well that species do not change of their own accord. Where are the proofs that species change? he demanded. How dare Darwin express such fanciful opinions without evidence to back them? How dare this man and his atheist followers take it on themselves to deny that God the Creator made man in His image and made all of the animals and all of the plants with a wisdom that man has no right to question?

This evolution idea, he continued, tells us that lowly forms of living things, such as cabbages and apes, are ever striving to change to become higher forms. (Darwin, of course, had never made such a claim.) Then he asked if anyone could accept the idea that a favored variety of turnip is tending to develop into men? Laughter.

Wilberforce was getting just the response he had wanted and felt that he had thoroughly smashed Darwin, through ridicule if not through reason. He next set about to discredit Darwin's champion, Huxley. Turning to Huxley, the Bishop said that evolutionists must be people who prefer to think that apes, not people, were their ancestors. Then he asked if it was through his grandmother or through his grandfather that Huxley claimed to be descended from the apes! The audience howled. Taking his seat, Wilberforce basked in their approval.

Huxley did not show any emotion. With calm assurance, he strode to the speaker's stand and began to systematically shatter every one of Wilberforce's shallow and slick arguments. Then in answer to the question about Huxley's ancestry, Huxley turned to the bishop and replied that if he were ever asked whether he would rather have a miserable ape for a grandfather, or a human being of high intelligence and high in office who chooses to use that intelligence and that office for the purpose of introducing ridicule into a serious scientific discussion, he would certainly choose the ape!

Wilberforce sat dumbfounded, not quite sure what had been said against him. But the audience had understood, and the uproar that followed was enough to convince Soapy Sam that he had been insulted and his arguments against evolution demolished.

Hooker's turn came next and Wilberforce nervously waited for the next blow. It came. Furious but in control, Hooker first exposed the shallow arguments of the bishop and then turned to points supporting evolution through natural selection. Soon he had the audience following his carefully reasoned arguments, and by the time he had finished there was no doubt that Darwinism had won the debate. Hooker wrote Darwin all about the meeting, which had taken four hours, saying that the battle had ended with no question of Darwin being left "master."

The Oxford debate created a climate of acceptance quickly. Scientists who before had only flipped through Darwin's book now studied it and followed its convincing arguments step by step. The idea of evolution by natural selection appealed especially to young scientists who felt restless and uncomfortable with the biblical account of the origin of life that met a dead end with Adam and Eve. *The Origin of Species* was translated into many foreign languages soon after it was published, and Darwin was delighted to receive numerous letters of praise from scientists the world over.

Darwin continued his work for another 20 years before he died in

1882. Although he knew that certain traits, certain variations are passed on from parent to offspring, he never came to know the biological details about how traits such as hair color or blood type, for example, were passed on. His theory further held that no two dogs, goldfish, fireflies, or people (except identical twins) are exactly alike and, therefore, have inherited different chances for survival. But how?

Before Darwin died, but unknown to him, the answers had begun to be worked out by an Austrian monk and plant scientist named Gregor Mendel. Although Mendel's work was published only six years after *The Origin of Species*, in 1865, it went unnoticed for 40 years. When Mendel's work was "discovered" soon after 1900, it quickly gave rise to the then new science of genetics.

What Mendel termed "units of inheritance" today are called genes. Recall that a gene is a certain region of that giant molecule of inheritance—DNA—we met in Chapter Three. Genes are what determine whether your eyes are blue or brown, that your blood type is O, and all the rest of your physical traits or characteristics. In a later chapter we will find out more about genes, how they sometimes get changed, and the role they play in evolution.

But now we will turn our attention to the fossil record and how paleontologists read it to learn about organic evolution through the ages.

6

Fossils and the Geologic Record

HOW FOSSILS ARE FORMED

Earth's rocky crust is a vast graveyard that contains the fossil remains of plants and animals that have lived throughout most of Earth's history, back to more than 3.5 billion years ago. The word *fossil* comes from the Latin word *fossilis,* which means "dug up." Fossils are the remains of plants and animals that were buried naturally. The sea floor is one of many places where fossils are formed. When fish and other marine animals die, their remains drift to the sea bottom where eventually they may be covered by an undersea mud slide. Over millions of years, the mud changes to rock, which may later be thrust up as a mountain. Or the sea may dry up, exposing its rock floor. Erosion by wind and rain then may wear away the rock and expose the fossil animal remains.

Soft-bodied animals such as jellyfish stand a poor chance of becoming fossils. Bone, shell, or hard wood, which don't decay very quickly, stand a much better chance. But hardness alone is not enough. The hard part must be buried before it can decay. Also, the plant or animal must remain rather undisturbed during the time it is becoming a fossil. Finally, to qualify as a fossil, the plant or animal remains usually must be at least 6,000 years old.

In a few unusual and rare cases, some very special condition has helped preserve almost the entire animal. Extreme cold or extreme dryness are such special conditions. Almost entire fossil mammoths have been found preserved in frozen ground, completely refrigerated for more than 25,000 years in Siberia and Alaska. And in dry regions of South America parts of mummified ground sloths have been found preserved in dry and protected caves. But these cases are rare.

Many of the plants and animals that are now part of the fossil record were preserved as their bone, shell, or other hard parts were changed into a different substance. Mineral-bearing water slowly seeping down through clay, mud, sand, or other sediments was soaked up by the porous bones, shell, or wood. As the water gradually evaporated, the minerals left behind filled the small open spaces within the bone or shell.

Brightly colored silica, calcite, or orange and red iron compounds often become part of fossil bone or shell. The addition of minerals tends to make the bone, shell, or wood even harder. Very often the actual bone or shell is dissolved by the ground water and is slowly replaced by the minerals in the water. In some petrified wood, silica has not only filled in small hollow spaces, but has replaced the once-living woody tissue. This has happened so perfectly that the individual cells and annual tree rings show up exactly millions of years later.

Many fossils are merely traces—impressions in stone—of past life. After the plant or animal died it was quickly buried in the sediments. Gradually the hard parts as well as the soft parts dissolved or decayed. Only a cavity or hollow space was left in the sedimentary rock where the shell or other hard part once lay. The walls of such cavities become a natural copy, or mold, of the shell or other skeletal part. Millions of years after the cavity is formed, minerals seep into and refill the cavity. In this way, a natural cast of the original mold is made, and centuries later may be dug up by a lucky fossil hunter. Molds and casts are very

Sometimes the bony part of an animal is gradually dissolved and replaced by minerals in the process of fossilization, as with these two coiled ammonites preserved in sedimentary rock. Ammonites evolved some 400 million years ago.

common fossil forms—especially for invertebrates, which are animals without backbones, such as clams and sponges.

Once in a while the hard outside skeleton and tiny legs of insects have been preserved in amber, the hardened and fossilized resin of ancient trees. Sandstone casts showing in remarkable detail the texture of dinosaur skin have been found in western Canada.

Sandstone, limestone (chalk), and shale are the chief fossil-bearing sedimentary rocks. They are soft, crumbly rock. The other two major rock types—igneous and metamorphic rock—seldom contain fossils. Igneous rock is hardened rock that flowed up from deeper parts of Earth's crust and solidified. Plant or animal remains that may be trapped by molten rock are almost always destroyed. Metamorphic rock is formed when great heat or pressure alters any other kind of rock. Once again, the heat nearly always destroys any plant or animal remains that may be trapped in the rock.

HOW FOSSILS ARE USED

All of our knowledge of past life is based on fossils and the rocks in which they are found. Fossils tell us that all present-day plants and animals have primitive ancestors that lived on Earth millions of years ago. And they are a record of what those plants and animals were like and how they lived.

Fossils also tell us something about the positions of seas and land masses of the past. By mapping the trail of marine fossils that mark the curving shoreline of an ancient inland sea, we can trace the outline of that sea. Two thousand years ago Greek scholars clearly saw in the fossil remains signs that land areas had sunk and risen at various times, but skeptics chose to believe that the fossils were only the remains of some "ancient worker's lunch." The trunks of fossilized trees found where they originally grew tell us of a former land area. We then know that an ancient sea did not cover that area at the time the trees were growing.

Paleontologists, scientists who study fossils, can also find out about the climate of past ages by studying fossils. What would you think if you found fossil tree ferns or fossil magnolias in Antarctica or Greenland? Such plants have been found in those places. You would have to conclude that the climate there had been much warmer, perhaps even a tropical climate, when those plants grew. Coal deposits often contain tree ferns and other plants. These plants suggest, again, that the region had been rather warm and swampy during the time the coal deposits were forming. But today many of these coal deposits are found in parts of the world that are quite cold and dry.

Fossils also give us clues about the age of the rocks that contain them. As early as the 1600s scientists knew that upper layers of rock were formed more recently and, therefore, had to be younger than rock layers lower down. In the early 1800s an English surveyor and engineer named William Smith built many canals. As he dug through the various rock layers he noticed that many of them contained fossils. He also noticed that any single rock layer usually had the same kinds of fossils. While the younger rock layers above each had one grouping, the older layers below contained different fossil groupings. Soon, Smith became so skillful an observer that whenever he saw a fossil he could tell from which layer of rock it had been collected.

At about the time of Smith's work, two French geologists were studying and mapping the fossil-bearing rock layers around Paris. Both Georges Cuvier and Alexandre Brongniart also noticed that certain types of fossils were found only in certain rock layers and not in others. As the two geologists arranged their collections of fossils in the same order as the rocks from which they came, they discovered something else—that the fossils changed in an orderly way from one layer to the next. The fossils from the higher and younger rock layers were more similar to modern forms of life than those fossils from the older rock layers deeper down. So, in an orderly column of fossil-bearing rock, it was possible to read the ways in which plants and animals had changed through many millions of years.

Over the years following the work of Smith, Cuvier, and Brongniart, information about the positions of fossils in the rock layers rapidly accumulated from all parts of the world. Today it is possible to place even a single kind of fossil from any part of the world into its proper time period.

Fossils, then, tell us two important things: 1) that certain kinds of plants and animals were living together during certain periods when certain sediments were forming; and 2) whether the sediments were formed on a shallow sea floor, in a desert, in a riverbed, or in a swamp.

By carefully studying fossils and the sedimentary rock that contains them, paleontologists can learn much about the past. They can, bit by bit, build up the setting for a giant and extinct reptile such as brontosaurus. They can tell what this dinosaur looked like, what animal neighbors it had, and what plants it ate, and they can describe the kinds of swamps in which it lived. In this way, paleontologists can call up scenes and events that occurred millions of years ago and so reconstruct certain aspects of Earth's past.

The occurrence of certain kinds of fossils in certain rock layers but

A great number of bones some 140 million years old have been excavated at Dinosaur National Monument in Colorado/Utah. Called the "sandbar cemetery," this fossil-rich area contains the petrified bones of crocodiles, turtles, and fourteen species of dinosaurs.

not in others seemed to say that at one period in Earth's history certain kinds of animals and plants existed for a time but then mysteriously died out as if some deathly plague had swept the land. Then in the overlying, younger rock layer new groups appeared that were not present earlier. Where did these new plant and animal species come from? And they, too, were to become extinct in later ages, for in still more recent rock layers not a trace of them was to be found. Entirely different species took their places. How could such observations be explained?

In the early 1800s Cuvier came up with an idea to account for the matter. From time to time, he said, a worldwide flood or some other catastrophic event wiped out most of the plants and animals then alive. His idea came to be called "catastrophism." Since Cuvier refused to believe that species evolve, he had to come up with some other way to account for the appearance of new species that replaced those wiped out. The only answer, he said, was that God kept creating new species to replace those He had destroyed. "Special creation" was the name given to this replacement of species. The ideas of catastrophism and special creation went hand in hand, seeming to explain everything about the origin of new species and the neatly layered fossil record simply and thoroughly.

However, those scientists who kept their religion separated from their science could not accept such an argument and warmly embraced the principle of evolution through natural selection to account for events revealed in the fossil record. That record has now been arranged in divisions similar to a yearly calendar.

THE GEOLOGIC CALENDAR
Scientists find it convenient to break Earth's history into small pieces, according to when certain kinds of plants and animals lived, when certain mountain ranges were thrust up, or when inland seas covered much of the continents from time to time. The time span we will use most often in this book is the geologic "period." Periods are grouped into larger time spans called "eras."

PRECAMBRIAN ERA

Precambrian means "before the Cambrian," and the era spans the time from Earth's formation 4.6 billion years ago to 580 million years ago. That amounts to 4 billion years, most of Earth's history to date. At the end of Chapter Three we left our story of evolution just as the Precambrian Era was drawing to a close.

PALEOZOIC ERA

The name of this era comes form the Greek words *palaios,* meaning "ancient," and *zoe,* meaning "life." The era spans 335 million years and contains six periods.

CAMBRIAN PERIOD   It is named after Cambria, the Roman name for Wales. The period lasted 80 million years, beginning 580 million years ago and ending 500 million years ago. The only plants and animals during this time lived in the seas, and none of the animals had backbones.

ORDOVICIAN PERIOD   It is named after an ancient Celtic tribe, the Ordovices, that lived in Wales. The period lasted 60 million years,

PRECAMBRIAN ERA	PALEOZOIC ERA				
Periods →	CAMBRIAN	ORDOVICIAN	SILURIAN	DEVONIAN	CARBONIFEROUS

4.6 billion years ago — 580 million — 500 million — 440 million — 400 million — 345 million — 290 million beginning 500 million years ago and ending 440 million years ago. Animals with backbones—including fish without jaws—evolved during the middle of this period.

SILURIAN PERIOD   It is named after the Silures, an ancient tribe in Wales. The period lasted 40 million years, beginning 440 million years ago and ending 400 million years ago. First plants, then later animals, took up life on the land. Among the plants were ferns; among the animals, millipedes.

DEVONIAN PERIOD   It is named after Devon, England. this period lasted 55 million years, beginning 400 million years ago and ending 345 million years ago. Because of the rapid evolution of fish, this period is known as the Age of Fishes. Amphibians evolved late in the period.

CARBONIFEROUS PERIOD   It is named for the extensive coal deposits formed during this time. The period lasted 55 million years, beginning 345 million years ago and ending 290 million years ago. Because of the rapid evolution of amphibians, animals that could live on land but spent part of their life cycles in water, this period is known

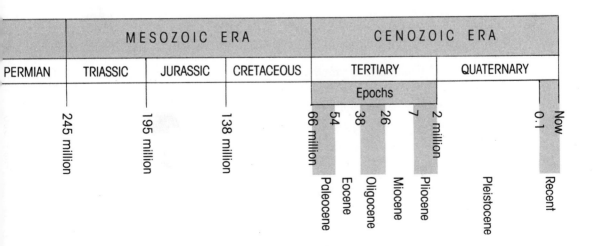

as the Age of Amphibians. The first reptiles evolved during the Carboniferous. This period sometimes is divided into two subperiods called the Mississippian and Pennsylvanian.

PERMIAN PERIOD   It is named after the province of Perm in the Ural Mountains of Russia. The period lasted 45 million years, beginning 290 million years ago and ending 245 million years ago. Conebearing trees, such as firs and spruce trees, were common. Change to a generally dry climate favored the evolution of reptiles over amphibians.

MESOZOIC ERA

The name of this era comes from the Greek words *mesos,* meaning "middle," and *zoe,* meaning "life." The era spans about 180 million years and contains three periods.

TRIASSIC PERIOD   The name is from the Latin word *trias,* meaning "three," and refers to a certain formation of rock in southern Germany. The period lasted 50 million years, beginning 245 million years ago and ending 195 million years ago. Earth's single supercontinent, called Pangaea, broke apart into a northern and a southern half. The ancestors of the dinosaurs evolved early in the period. The dinosaurs evolved late in the period.

JURASSIC PERIOD   It is named after the Jura Mountains of France and Switzerland. The period lasted 57 million years, beginning 195 million years ago and ending 138 million years ago. Because of the success of the dinosaurs, this period is called the Age of Reptiles. Feathered birds and the first mammals, about the size of a rat, evolved during the Jurassic.

CRETACEOUS PERIOD   The name is from the Latin word *creta,* meaning "chalk." The period lasted 72 million years, beginning 138 million years ago and ending about 66 million years ago. Flowering plants had evolved and were common. The dinosaurs became extinct, as did many other animal species, in a mass dying. The continents began to take on their present-day shapes during this period.

CENOZOIC ERA

The name for this era comes from the Greek words *kainos,* meaning "recent," and from *zoe,* meaning "life." The era spans about 65 million years and contains two periods.

TERTIARY PERIOD   This period lasted 64 million years, beginning 66 million years ago and ending two million years ago. A general cooling, coupled with the widespread extinction of many reptile species, favored the rapid evolution of mammals. By the late Tertiary, most modern-day birds had evolved, as had many mammal groups including cats, whales, and, late in the period, mammoths, mastodons, giant bison, 7-foot-long beavers. This and the next period together are called the Age of Mammals.

QUATERNARY PERIOD   This period spans the most recent two million years of Earth's history. Modern horses evolved early in the period, as did several humanlike types, of which we are the sole survivors. Massive glaciers covered much of North America and northern Europe off and on during this period, with the last ice age ending about 10,000 years ago. The ice ages wiped out many mammal species, especially the giant ones.

A different period division for the Cenozoic is sometimes used. It includes the Paleogene Period, which lasted from about 65 to 26 million years ago, and the Neogene Period, which lasted from 26 million years ago to the present.

The fossil record shows that uncountable numbers of species have come and gone throughout Earth's geologic history. As species become extinct because of changes in the environment, new species better equipped to cope with those environmental changes have evolved and filled the ecological nooks.

What we will do next is take a closer look at the biological events that give rise to new species—mutation, variation, and adaptation.

The more the secrets of Nature are probed,
the greater the wonder that they instill.
—Sir Gavin de Beer, 1964

7

Genes and Populations

THE "MAGIC" OF MUTATION

In Chapter Four we talked about mutations. A mutation comes about when a link in the chain of molecules making a strand of DNA is changed in some way. Maybe a bond holding two atoms together is broken, or maybe a bond is added where it is not needed. Or two links in a strand of DNA may get reversed. Such a change in DNA is a mutation.

Mutations are regularly caused by radiation, either natural radiation from the Sun or from minerals in the soil, or radiation produced by human beings in nuclear bomb tests or as nuclear wastes. Mutations also may be caused by certain harmful chemicals that we release into the environment as pollution, and sometimes they may be caused by heat. Mutations also may result from "mistakes" made when our cells divide and make new cells. A mutation happens whenever the DNA made for the new cell is not an exact copy of the original DNA molecule.

As you know from Chapter Four, most mutations are harmful. Often they are deadly. In human beings mutations cause more than one thousand hereditary disorders. What happens is that one or more mutant genes give instructions to RNA to make the wrong kind of protein, which prevents the liver, blood, or some other organ or tissue from working just the way it should.

Dwarfs have one or more mutant genes that prevent them from developing into full-size human beings. Color blindness also is caused by a mutation, as are albinism, hemophilia, cystic fibrosis, and muscular dystrophy. A person with albinism, called an albino, has white hair, pink eyes, and lacks the brown pigment (melanin) in the skin that helps screen out the ultraviolet, or sunburning, rays. Because albinos lack the pigment, they are very sensitive to sunburn and must be very careful

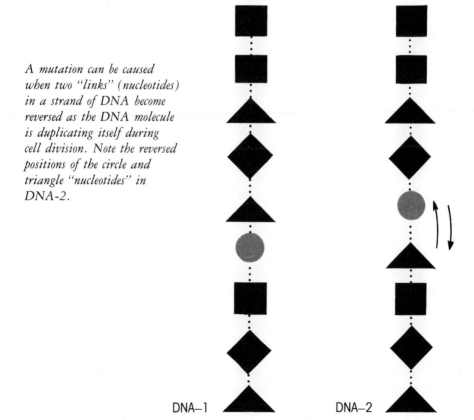

A mutation can be caused when two "links" (nucleotides) in a strand of DNA become reversed as the DNA molecule is duplicating itself during cell division. Note the reversed positions of the circle and triangle "nucleotides" in DNA-2.

DNA—1

DNA—2

about exposing themselves to the Sun. Hemophilia disrupts formation of the protein that stops the bleeding when you cut your finger, for example. People with this mutation are called "bleeders" and must be especially careful to avoid any injury that can cause bleeding.

Although nearly all mutations are harmful, some are helpful. And those are the ones that are the driving force of evolution. For example, some 8,000 or more years ago, people would lose the ability to digest the sugar lactose in milk once they became adults. Then a mutation occurred that enabled a child to continue the digestion of lactose into adulthood. The mutant genes responsible were then passed on from parent to offspring and spread among populations in and around the Middle East those 8,000 years ago. This mutation changed the course of history by encouraging the breeding of milk cows, the milking of goats and sheep, and the production of cheese, butter, and other milk products simply because adults had biologically "learned" to digest lactose. The ability to digest milk products provided a valuable new source of nutrition—animal protein without the need to kill the animal. It also provided a source of vitamin D. However, in certain parts of the world today infants, children, and adults who do not benefit from the mutation are unable to digest lactose.

When we consider a mutation being passed on from parent to offspring, we must imagine our bodies as having only two main kinds of cells. One consists of the cells of our skin, heart, blood, and other body parts. Although mutations occur in these cells, the mutations are never passed on from parent to offspring. Mutations can be passed along only through the second main kind of cell: the egg cells produced by females and sperm cells produced by males. Those cells are our reproductive cells, also called sex cells, or gametes.

HOW MUTATIONS CAUSE VARIATION

When a human sperm cell of a male joins with an egg cell of a female, the resulting new cell usually develops into a baby. Because the egg cell contains the mother's DNA, or genes, and because the sperm cell contains the father's, the baby has DNA from both of its parents. That is why

MALE SEX CELL (SPERM)   FEMALE SEX CELL (EGG)

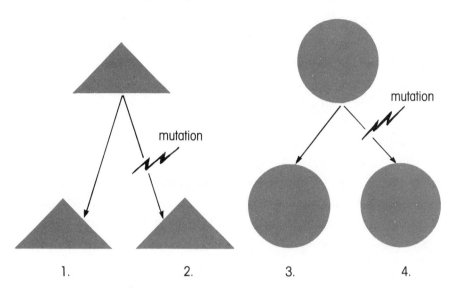

1.   2.   3.   4.

How mutations in the sex cells (gametes) of a male and female parent can be passed on to their children: If a normal sperm cell (1) fertilizes a normal egg cell (3), the child receives no new genes, only those of its parents. However, if a normal sperm cell (1) fertilizes a mutant egg cell (4), the child receives one new gene from its mother. If a mutant sperm cell (2) fertilizes a normal egg cell (3), the child also receives one new gene, this time from its father. But if a mutant sperm cell (2) fertilizes a mutant egg cell (4), the child receives two new genes, one each from the father and mother. Because about 50 percent of all gametes have one new gene through mutation, 75 percent of offspring have new genes.

we sometimes say that Suzie "has her mother's eyes" or "her father's smile" or "her grandmother's hair color."

But while Suzie is a mixture of both her parents, she also has characteristics of her very own that her parental stock lacks. She may be taller or especially well coordinated. Some such differences in Suzie come from genetic "mistakes" made when DNA of her mother combined with that of her father, then recombined and formed Suzie. Paired DNA strands often do not separate cleanly. Instead, they may swap certain genes, providing Suzie with new gene segments that were not present in either parent. In other words, certain of Suzie's parents' genes have been reshuffled and have given Suzie certain characteristics that neither her mother nor her father has. Called recombination, this reshuffling of genes during DNA copying in sex cells is another important cause of variation in a population's gene pool.

So each offspring produced by sexual reproduction—an elm tree, a spider, or a human being—inherits characteristics through the DNA of both of its parents. Because a new individual develops from its parents' gametes—and not from the body cells—only the gene mutations and recombinations of the gametes can be passed on from parent to offspring. Genetic recombination is by far the most important source of variation.

Mutations happen to certain genes more often than to others, and only recently have biologists begun to learn just how often certain mutations occur in human beings. For instance, the mutation that produces dwarfs occurs forty-one times in every million gametes. The mutation for albinism and that for complete color blindness occur twenty-eight times in every million gametes.

Biologists think that perhaps 50 percent of all gametes produced by a person have at least one new mutated gene. Those mutations are the raw materials of the many differences among your friends and among all the individuals in any population of people, dogs, cows, or other organisms. Those individual differences among us—long legs, short fingers, red hair—are what we call genetic variation. Without such variation we would all tend to be pretty much alike. Changing patterns of variation in a population provide the driving force of evolution.

HOW GENES GET AROUND

How do genes spread through a population? To start off with a simple example, let's imagine a population of thirty mice in a laboratory. Let's further imagine that our mice vary in only a few ways. Some have short ears, others long ears. Some have long tails, others short tails. Some have straight hair, others have curly hair. Some are white, others gray. Those are the only variations in the population, and each variation is controlled by a single gene. The mice are exactly alike in all other ways.

So a total of eight genes control a total of eight variations. Again, to keep our example simple, we will say that a total of one hundred additional genes account for all other traits that make the mice exactly alike in all other ways. So the grand total of different kinds of genes available to the population of mice is 108. That collection of genes in the population is called the population's gene pool.

If we were able to prevent mutations from occurring in the population of mice as they reproduced, the population would grow larger but variation would forever be limited to only certain combinations of traits in new offspring.

A new individual could be

> long eared, long tailed, straight haired, and white
> or long eared, long tailed, straight haired, and gray
> or long eared, long tailed, curly haired, and gray
> or long eared, short tailed, curly haired, and gray
> or short eared, short tailed, curly haired, and gray
> or short eared, short tailed, curly haired and white

and so on until all possible combinations were reached.

Now suppose that a mutation affected the population by eliminating all curly-haired varieties. How would that change the "look" of the population? Suppose further that another mutation produced claws on toes. How many new variants would that produce?

If you decide to complete this exercise you may be surprised how much variation could result in the mouse population with only eight simple variations at the beginning, and then with the added variation of claws. But in an actual population of animals in nature mutations produce thousands upon thousands of variations. So the gene pool of any natural population contains millions of genes available to be exchanged as new offspring are born, not only 108.

HOW VARIATION HELPS POPULATIONS ADAPT

The ability of any population in nature to be in tune with its environment at a given time, and to adjust, or adapt, to changes in the environment, depends on variation among the individuals making up the population.

Variation, in turn, depends on mutation. Variation among individuals expresses itself in many ways—an animal's behavior, its appearance, and its physical makeup. For example, some individuals are better at finding food during hard times; others are better at withstanding the cold or the heat; some are swifter in escaping predators or catching prey; others are smarter at solving problems, and so on.

If the climate turns cold, those individuals who can withstand the cold survive, and those who can't withstand the cold die. Those who survive, mate and pass their "cold-survival" genes on to their offspring and into the population's gene pool. Gradually the population changes as the less fit individuals are weeded out by natural selection while the more fit individuals survive. And the more fit individuals are the ones who, by reproducing, keep adding their fitter genes to the population's gene pool. Through the process of beneficial change in the gene pool, a population adapts to changes in its environment.

Again, Darwin's idea of "survival of the fittest" is the key thought here. Change in the gene pool of a population, and the buildup of beneficial genes, is evolution through natural selection, and it happens on the level of populations, not on the level of individuals. Evolution is not the ability of a wolf to change into a dog or an ape to change into a human being. Instead, it is the gradual change in a population, usually over millions of years, resulting from environmental change that favors certain variations and doesn't favor certain others. If you understand the facts in this paragraph and the two paragraphs before it, you are well on the way to understanding how evolution works.

An interesting example of how a change in the environment favors certain variations and not others occurred in England in the mid-1800s. At that time there were two varieties of the moth species, *Biston betularia,* which is a favorite food of certain birds. The most numerous variety had light-colored wings, while a mutant variety in far fewer numbers had dark-colored wings. But then over a period of about 50 years, the light-colored variety began to disappear; by 1895 about 98 percent of the moth population around the city of Manchester was dark colored. What caused the change?

During that period of 50 years, the environment around Manchester changed in a way important to the moths. An increase in the number of factories burning coal darkened the ground and vegetation with soot. Before this happened the light-colored moths blended into the background of leaves and tree bark. The birds that fed on them had trouble finding them, and so they were protected. However, the dark-colored moths stood out and were easy targets for birds. The variation of light color was an important adaptation for the survival of the population of mostly light-colored moths.

But with the darkening of the landscape, it was the light-colored individuals that stood out and became easy targets for birds. The dark-winged individuals now were protected by camouflage. Gradually the population's gene pool came to contain far more genes for dark coloration than for light coloration because an increasing number of dark-winged individuals were surviving and producing offspring. The population adapted through natural selection to a change in the environment, with the "fittest" individuals surviving and passing on their dark-wing fitness to the population's offspring and so increasing the number of beneficial genes in the gene pool.

You have just seen one way in which the gene pool of a population can be changed. There are other ways. One is called gene flow and comes about when individuals from one population move away and join a population adapted to a slightly different environment. When immigrant individuals of a dark-skinned population, for example, mate with light-skinned members of the resident population, a flow of genes for dark skin occurs. New gene combinations result and add to the population's gene pool, increasing variation in the population.

Another way a population's gene pool can change is through genetic drift. This happens when many individuals of a population of alpine butterflies, for example, are killed by a particularly harsh winter. The gene pool is seriously drained, and the few remaining individuals have fewer genes and gene combinations available as they rebuild their population.

A special case of genetic drift involves a small religious sect called the Dunkers who live in eastern Pennsylvania. More than 200 years ago a small group of Dunkers came to America from western Germany and ever since have clung to their customs, one of which prohibits marriage with outsiders. Nearly ten generations of maintaining a small gene pool have led to a number of interesting genetic traits. For instance, when compared with their relatives in Germany and with the general population in the United States, the Dunkers have very few individuals with either B or AB blood types. The gene controlling those blood types has been nearly lost and never reintroduced into their gene pool.

HOW SPECIES CHANGE

You'll recall that we defined a species as any population whose individual members look pretty much alike, who can mate and produce offspring, and whose offspring in turn can have offspring.

Sometimes a population gets broken into two isolated groups. If the groups stay separate, eventually the gene pool of each will change enough to prevent successful mating between members of the two groups. According to our definition, the two groups will have become different species. It may take about 50,000 years to accomplish, but both groups will evolve gene pools that will be markedly different from each other.

There have been cases of isolated populations of fruit flies evolving differences in their reproductive organs so that members of two neighboring populations could no longer mate. The same has been true of isolated populations of salamanders. In the case of plants, two isolated populations of a certain species of flowering plant may each follow a new and different genetic course, which will lead to a new species. This could happen if one of the populations continued to produce flowers in June but the other one flowered in August. Since their flowering times would be different, there would be no possibility for the two populations to combine the sex cells of their flowers and produce offspring. The longer any two populations of plants or animals remain isolated from each other in different environments, the greater the differences between them become.

A well-studied example of new species in the making involves the common leopard frog, which lives in widely differing environments stretching all the way from Mexico to Vermont. The closer any two populations are to each other, the more alike are their gene pools. But the farther apart two populations are, the less alike are their gene pools and the less likely the ability to mate successfully. One of the chief rules for speciation, or the making of a new species, is that the isolated populations adapt to environments that are markedly different from each other.

While changes leading to an inability to produce offspring among members of two isolated populations may be occurring, other changes may also occur—changes in tooth shape and size, blood type, nose shape, wing length, for example. Over hundreds of thousands of years, members of related but isolated populations may not only lose the ability to mate and produce offspring but may become quite different from each other in appearance or behavior as well.

An understanding of how species change is essential to an understanding of how evolution works. We can now define evolution as those changes in a population's gene pool that make the population ever better adapted to its environment. In addition to favoring genes that are beneficial and make a population more fit, evolution at the same time tends to weed out from the gene pool those individuals whose genes are harmful to the population.

We had stumbled on a little window into time, a window that gave us a peek at what was going on in an ancient sea some 55 million years ago. Such glimpses never fail to get me going. For life has had a history, just as human civilization has had a history.

—Niles Eldredge, 1987

8

Climbing the Tree of Evolution

SOFT COATS AND "MISSING LINKS"

We will now pick up the story of evolution where we left it at the end of Chapter Four and near the beginning of the Cambrian Period, about 580 million years ago. By the beginning of Cambrian times, soft-bodied sea-dwelling organisms that had evolved some 90 million years earlier had given rise to numerous new and increasingly complex forms.

In the 1700s and 1800s so many fossils of so many different kinds of plants and animals were being found in Cambrian-age rocks the world over that many biologists began to think that life itself arose only at the beginning of the Cambrian. Although life had not yet taken to the land, Cambrian seas abounded with plants, numerous soft-bodied animals such as sponges, and other animals with hard outer coats such as the trilobites.

Not until fairly recent times did paleontologists uncover earlier fossils of soft-bodied animals from the late Precambrian, as well as microfossils of bacteria from an even earlier time that proved that cellular life abounded at least 3.5 billion years ago.

Around 1950 paleontologists digging in Cambrian-age rocks of the Ediacara Hills in Australia discovered unusual fossil impressions that radioactive "clocks" dated at about 670 million years old. These fossils were unusual in that they did not resemble the multitude of animals that evolved at the beginning of the Cambrian. One rule in evolution is that plants or animals closely related in time usually are closely related in body plan and function. Not so with the late Precambrian Ediacara Hills fossils compared with their Cambrian descendants.

Among the oddball fossils were coral-type animals, but lacking a protective house of calcium shell. There were also wormlike critters, jellyfish, and many puzzling animals unlike anything we know. One wormlike form *(Spriggina)* had a head region, suggesting that it may have been an ancestor of the trilobites that abounded during the Cambrian. None of the Ediacaran fossils had hard parts; all were soft bodied, which explains why so few of them have been discovered. On dying, relatively few of the Precambrian animals remained in one piece long enough to become fossils before becoming dinner for bacteria.

Where are the "missing links" that would form a smooth and gradual change between the late Precambrian and early Cambrian marine animals? Usually we are told that that is the way evolution proceeds—smoothly with gradual changes over long periods of time, and following a straight path from simple to ever more complex forms. But, as mentioned earlier, many biologists now think that evolution need not follow that route in all cases. They say that major changes in body plan and function have taken place through adaptation and given rise to new species over relatively short periods of time. We will have more to say about this new idea toward the end of this chapter. For now it is enough to realize that relatively simple life in the form of bacteria was the rule almost up to the Cambrian Period, then as if by magic the numerous complex forms of the Cambrian flowered in only a few million years.

HARD COATS AND SHELLS OF THE CAMBRIAN

The major thing that marks the Cambrian as different from the Precambrian is the evolution of many animals with protective coats of shell and other hard parts that served as armor against the waves of their ocean home and against predators. Some hard parts were composed of calcium carbonate, others of calcium phosphate, and others of chitin. Chitin is the organic material that forms the armor coating of grasshoppers.

During the entire 80 million years of the Cambrian Period, the many new species that evolved all lived in warm, shallow seas. Because they lacked backbones, they are called invertebrates. Plants and animals were not to take up life on the land for nearly another 200 million years.

Kings of the Cambrian seas were the trilobites, which make up about 70 percent of the Cambrian fossil record. For that reason, the Cambrian might well be called the Age of Trilobites. Their species numbered in the thousands and they were everywhere. Most were about 2 inches long, although some were as large as a computer screen. Some swam, others walked over the sea floor or burrowed in the mud. Some had well-developed eyes, others lacked eyes. None had jaws or teeth. As

Hard-shelled sea animals called trilobites crowded Cambrian seas and came in near-limitless varieties. Their hard shells and great numbers made them ideal candidates for fossilization.

they grew, trilobites shed their chitin shells in a process called molting and made larger shells after each shedding. Considering their great numbers in the Cambrian, and the fact that they could exist without their shells between molts, they most likely had soft-bodied ancestors back in the Precambrian.

The trilobites were to give rise, much later, to today's crabs, lobsters, shrimps, spiders, and insects. All belong to that animal group (phylum) called arthropods, all of which have jointed legs and make up about 80 percent of all animals.

Had you been a scuba diver of those ancient Cambrian seas, you would have seen many strange, wonderful, and frightening things. Sharing those seas with the trilobites were eurypterids, giant "sea scorpions" about 10 feet long, now extinct. There were also brachiopods, clamlike animals with two shells. But unlike today's clams, they lived attached to the sea floor and captured drifting food with hairlike tentacles. While many Cambrian animals grazed on colonies of algae, many others were predators.

Another animal group that was well represented during the Cambrian is called echinoderms, meaning "spiny skin" because pointed knobs of their skeletons stick out through their skin. Echinoderms include present-day starfish, brittle stars, sea urchins, sand dollars, sea cucumbers, and sea lilies. Sea lilies, with their long stalked bodies and feathery arms that wave back and forth in the current, look more like plants than animals. None of these animals has what you would term a head, and all are built on a five-part body plan, each part directed outward from a common center. Some of the Cambrian echinoderms moved about freely while others were rooted in the sea floor or cemented to the shells of other animals.

The first reefs were built during the Cambrian by mysterious organisms called archeocyathids. Their small soft bodies grew within hard cones that often clustered in colonies and formed reef mounds. None of the Cambrian animals came even close to looking like their modern-day descendants.

Crinoids, or sea lilies, lived attached to the sea floor and spanned several geologic time periods. The crinoid fossil here is about 200 million years old.

Why the sudden evolutionary explosion of animals with hard parts as opposed to the soft-bodied types? Competition and survival are the answers. With more and more new types of Cambrian sea life evolving to fill every available environmental corner, mutations producing protective armor were favored, and populations lucky enough to acquire hard outer parts were most likely to prosper. As more and more such species evolved, the remaining soft-bodied species were at a dangerous disadvantage and most quickly became extinct. Those that were not eaten alive by hard-shelled predators often were devoured after death by scavengers and so didn't survive to become fossils.

One of the richest Cambrian fossil deposits is one called the Burgess Shale. It was discovered in 1910 near Field, British Columbia, in the Canadian Rockies. Over the 10-year period following its discovery, more than thirty-five thousand Cambrian fossils were found and sent to various museums for study.

The continents during the Cambrian did not in the least resemble those on a modern-day globe. There was an enormous land mass called Gondwana, which much later was to break up into smaller land masses including Africa, South America, India, Australia, and Antarctica.

Before the Triassic Period, about 245 million years ago, Earth is thought to have had only a single supercontinent called Pangaea. During the Triassic, Pangaea broke apart into two major continents, one in the south called Gondwana, the other in the north called Laurasia.

Gondwana means "land of the Gonds," a people living in present-day India. A second major land mass called Laurasia included what was later to become Eurasia, North America, Greenland, and Scotland.

During the early Cambrian, shallow seas covered large areas of the edges of the land masses that then existed. Later during the period the seas spread inland. All the while, sand, clay, and other sediments were being washed into those seas and filling long underwater ditches. Eventually, two of those sediment dumps on Laurasia were thrust up as the mountain ranges we know today as the Rocky Mountains and the Appalachians. So those two mighty ranges had their beginnings long ago in the Cambrian Period, although the Rockies are much younger than the Appalachians.

There were several mass extinctions of trilobites that lived in the warm tropical seas of Laurasia. But after each mass extinction, many new species evolved and competed for the environmental pastures vacated by the species that had become extinct. No one knows the cause of the mass extinctions, but there are a few educated guesses. Among them is temperature change.

Possibly a temporary chilling of the warm, shallow seas wiped out numerous temperature-sensitive species over a period of only a few thousand years. There were, however, certain other hardy species adapted to life in cool, deep water that thrived in the cooling seas. Over a few million years those species occupied the many environmental nooks and crannies left by the species that had become extinct.

We saw an example of just such evolution—called adaptive radiation—in the chapter describing Darwin's finches. Populations of a given trilobite species would branch out, each moving into a slightly different cold-water environment and adapting to it. In time, the new adaptations of those populations changed them into new trilobite species. The North American fossil record clearly shows that several such mass extinctions of trilobites took place and that numerous new trilobite species filled the ecological vacant lots through adaptive radiation.

Of the thousands of Cambrian species known to have existed, not

Ordovician seas teemed with cephalopods, animals that lived in long, coiled shells. Today's octopuses and squids are relatives of the early cephalopods. Ordovician seas also contained trilobites, bryozoans, brachiopods, graptolites, and crinoids.

a single one survives today. Individuals die and species become extinct, but life goes on.

THE ORDOVICIAN PERIOD

Evolution during the next geologic period, the Ordovician, gave rise to many hard-shelled invertebrates that came to outnumber the trilobites. Among them were the hard-shelled brachiopods and bryozoans, or moss animals, made up of colonies of brachiopodlike animals, as well as clams and many corals. There also were crinoids, or sea lilies, which lived attached to the sea bottom, and numerous and highly successful cephalopods, meaning "head-foot."

Some cephalopods of the time lived in coiled shells, others in long, cone-shaped shells. When young, a cephalopod lived in a small, simple shell chamber. But as it outgrew its chamber it formed a new and larger one. So it kept adding new chambers and growing into them until the train of chambers became quite long. Today, cephalopods are the most highly developed of all the mollusks. In all, there have been about ten thousand species of cephalopods, and about four hundred species are alive today, including octopuses and squids.

During the middle of the Ordovician—about 450 million years ago—an important new animal type evolved. It was the first of the fish. Lacking jaws, it was not much like the salmon, sole, or other fish of our dinner table today. And Colorado sandstone of middle Ordovician age contains tiny scraps of bony plates thought to be the earliest known remains of animals with a backbone, the vertebrates. If they are the earliest vertebrates, they are the ancestors of all of today's mammals, birds, reptiles, amphibians, and true fish.

THE SILURIAN PERIOD

Most of the land area of today's Northern Hemisphere continued to be covered by shallow seas during the Silurian Period, which followed the Ordovician and lasted about 40 million years. The highly successful trilobites, numerous for more than 150 million years, began to die out in large numbers, and vertebrate species increased. Many of these early animals with backbones had bony armor as protection against predators. Others had thick protective scales. Giant water scorpions 10 feet long were common.

Far better fossils of animals with backbones are found for this period than for the Ordovician, but none had yet developed jaws. They were either surface feeders or bottom feeders that used tentacles to catch passing food or sucked in food vaccuum-cleaner fashion. Near the end of the Silurian, however, new types of backboned animals were evolving: the placoderms, fish with jaws capable of biting, cutting, and crushing prey. This new feature made the placoderms especially successful predators.

During the Silurian, life seems to have taken its first hold in the hostile environment of the land. By this time weathering of the rocky surface had formed soil, a new medium for experiments in evolution and one that proved suitable for plants. Recall from Chapter Four that "animal" cells evolved ahead of plants during the Age of Bacteria, but plants became the first life forms to make a living on the land

The earliest known fossils of land plants have been found in Silurian rocks from Australia and Europe. Called psilopsids, they are a group that has survived up to the present time. These leafless plants most likely were shallow-water types that gradually evolved features enabling them to survive as the level of the seas lowered from time to time. Photosynthesis in these leafless plants took place in their stems, which contained a rich supply of those green structures called chloroplasts that are needed for photosynthesis. Later, ferns evolved and became abundant as early land plants.

Animal life also seems to have taken hold on the land during the late Silurian. The earliest forms yet identified are millipedes and scorpionlike organisms such as those air-breathers found preserved in later Silurian rocks from Scotland. Both probably were scavengers, eating the remains of marine organisms stranded on the beach at high tide or during storms.

In this period there was much volcanic activity in what is now Maine and the Canadian areas of New Brunswick and eastern Quebec. Other land disturbances gave rise to a 4,000-mile-long mountain range extending from Wales through Scandinavia and westward to northern Greenland. At this time, it would have been possible to walk from Canada to Europe since there was no Atlantic Ocean.

The Cambrian, Ordovician, and Silurian periods are grouped together as the Paleozoic Era. Climate during the Paleozoic seems to have been generally mild, as we can tell from the distribution of fossils. Early Paleozoic fossils found north of the Arctic Circle differ very little from those found near the Equator, and fossils of the same species are found rather widely spread both north and south, just as if there had been hardly any difference in climate in what is now southern South America and midlatitude Canada.

THE DEVONIAN: THE AGE OF FISHES

The Age of Fishes is the name given to the Devonian Period because fish evolved into a bewildering variety of forms. Their speed gave them an advantage in catching prey and escaping predators. Many were armored like their Silurian ancestors; others were covered with small scales. And compared with the speedsters, still others were sluggish.

One of the most fearsome of the fish was a group called the arthrodires, which were 20 to 30 feet long. They had vicious shearing jaws and heads encased in bony armor. The arthrodires appeared in the early Devonian, evolved rapidly, and then became extinct by the end of the period.

Devonian fish included two newcomers. One was the ancestor of modern sharks, and the other was the ancestor of the bony fish that play an important part in our diet today. Some of the Devonian bony fish had an air bladder that worked as a kind of lung and enabled the fish to gulp air. They were the lungfish.

Lungfish were highly successful during the mid to late Devonian times, as was another mid-Devonian newcomer called a coelacanth. In 1938 a fisherman dredged up what later came to be called a "living fossil" off the coast of South Africa. It was a living fish about 4 feet long, with a broad tail and coarse scales. When biologists examined it, they identified it as a coelacanth, a close descendant of a fish type that evolved during the mid-Devonian, some 420 million years ago. Since 1938 several coelacanths have been caught off the Comoro Islands north of Madagascar.

Like the Devonian coelacanths, the lungfish also have present-day look-alike descendants. Another "living fossil" is the modern horseshoe crab, a look-alike descendant of Paleozoic sea scorpions. One reason these so-called living fossils interest us is that they break the rule that evolution usually produces changes in body plan. Living fossils belong to groups that have tended to produce related look-alike species rather than related but rather different-appearing species. How can we account for this?

Some biologists suspect that living fossils so closely resemble their ancient ancestors because the gene pools of the ancestral species were

Middle Devonian seas had many coral reefs. The flowerlike shapes are the tentacle-rimmed mouths of corals. There also were sponges, starfish, mollusks, and stalked plantlike animals called sea lilies. The long, tubular cephalopods were still around, as were trilobites.

poor in variation and so kept the descendant species in an anatomical straitjacket. Other biologists think that if the environment of a long line of living fossils remains pretty much the same—as in the case of the deep-ocean-dwelling coelacanth—then natural selection keeps the animal or plant members of the long line looking pretty much the same. Biologists term this evolutionary lag "arrested evolution." At first glance, this may seem to be a good explanation, but then how do we account for the fact that many animal and plant groups do go through major evolutionary changes even though they live in environments that change little? It's a puzzle.

As a rule, plant and animal species that make the oceans their home evolve more slowly than plants and animals that live on the land. Again, at least part of the explanation seems to be that the ocean environment tends to be more stable, less changing than the land environment. Recall that it is environmental change that causes the widespread extinction of species and so opens many new environmental nooks and crannies to be occupied by new species.

Niles Eldredge, of New York's American Museum of Natural History, speaks of "ecological generalists" and "ecological specialists." In an animal or plant group that is made up of many different species, each species tends to be specialized and very particular about its environment. Darwin's finches are an example. Ecological specialists may eat only certain types of food, be sensitive to a narrow temperature range, and so on. An extreme example is the silkworm. It eats only the leaves of mulberry bushes, and if its eggs are not laid on a mulberry plant, the larval hatchlings starve to death.

The ecological generalists are less fussy about life. They eat several different food types, can stand relatively large changes in temperature, and so on. In Eldredge's words, they tend to be "jacks-of-all-trades" and as a result of not becoming "advanced" through specialization of body plan and living habits stand a better chance of surviving in the face of environmental change. Such "primitive" groups of generalists tend to evolve more slowly than the more "advanced" specialists.

The adaptation of animals to life on land can be seen as an engineering problem of daunting proportions, comparable in complexity to human beings living on other planets.
—*Lynn Margulis, 1986*

9

The Challenge of Life on Land

FROM LUNGFISH TO AMPHIBIANS

By the middle Devonian, plants had become well rooted on the land. Possibly the first land plant populations took up life in tidal zones where they spent some of the time under water and some exposed to the air. Then some groups were able to spend most or all of their time on land, taking in water through roots. By mid-Devonian times, after having carried out experiments in evolution for many millions of years, land plants had become well established far inland and were plentiful enough to leave fossils in the form of driftwood.

Then one day a group of vertebrates decided to go ashore and take up life on the land also. It didn't happen quite that way, but the effect was the same. Among the star performers on the Devonian stage of evolution were the lobe-finned fish, or crossopterygians, which were different from other fish groups in two important ways. First, in addition to gills, which enabled them to "breathe" in water, they had an air

The lobe-finned fishes of the Devonian spent part of their time on the land. A special bladder enabled them to gulp air for breathing when out of water, and they could move about by pushing and pulling themselves over the mud with muscular lobes that served as primitive "feet." This reconstruction shows a cros-sopterygian, "Eusthenopteron."

bladder that worked as a kind of lung. These fish could rise to the surface and gulp air and so get oxygen that way as well as from the water. Second, they had a muscular lobe at the end of each powerful fin. Each lobe contained bony structures that could be moved into different po-sitions and so be used to push and pull the fish over mud flats. The combination of lungs and lobe-fins also enabled these fish to remain alive during times of drought. They could dig into the mud and wait there for the return of water, just as modern lungfish do to this day.

What made the lobe-fins take to the land is not entirely clear. Possibly their populations swelled to such great numbers that their shallow-water habitats became fouled and they crawled overland in search of better water holes. And possibly seasonal drought sent them off in search of new water-homes. So the first vertebrates to take up life on the land may not have been adventurers at all but simply fish in need of a better water hole.

It would be a mistake to suppose that the lobe-fins evolved lungs and lobes *in order to* take up life on the land. Those two adaptations persisted simply because they were useful and necessary in a watery habitat. The fact that they turned out to be useful in a land habitat was nothing more than a stroke of good luck. There is no foresight or design in natural selection, any more than there is purpose. Natural selection favors a trait only because it is useful to an organism in its present environment. That is important to understand.

One advantage the early land-dwelling animals had was a lack of competition. There were no predators to track them down as food, and those who were able to eat plants as a steady diet had endless and rich pastures, since plants had already become established on the land. But taking up life on the land posed problems. One was an engineering problem that required a rebuilt muscular system and improved skeletal system to support the lobe-fins on land, when they were not buoyed up as they were in water. A way to cope with a much richer oxygen supply also had to be found. And special coats of skin or other material were needed for two reasons: first, to protect the animal from the fierce direct rays of the Sun; and second, to hold in the watery environment that kept the animal's tissues alive.

To this day every living animal carries within it a small amount of the ocean in which animal life originated. The amounts of salts in our blood are almost identical to those in seawater, as are the proportions of elements including sodium, potassium, and chloride in our tissues. As

Margulis has put it, "No animal has ever really completely left the watery microcosm. . . . We sweat and cry what is basically seawater."

The lobe-fins were an evolutionary bridge between the fish and the next major group of animals—the amphibians. The amphibians were well established on land by the end of the Devonian and reached their peak some 310 million years ago in the many swamps of the Carboniferous landscape. Their bodies were slim, they had fishlike tails and were four-footed. One of the first amphibians was *Ichthyostega,* whose fossil remains have been found in Greenland and who might be described as a crossopterygian fish with big feet.

In 1988 scientists working in Iowa dug up the oldest well-preserved land vertebrate known to exist in North America. It is an early amphibian 335 million years old. Although adapted to life on the land, the three-to five-foot-long animal resembling a giant salamander probably spent most of its time in the water.

All during the Carboniferous and into the next period, the Permian, the amphibians had the world to themselves. With little competition, their species came in many sizes, shapes, and ways of life. While some were small and snakelike, others looked something like alligators. Some were meat-eaters and had sharp pointed teeth with which to kill prey, but they lacked cutting teeth and powerful jaws, so they had to swallow prey whole. Others were bulky plant-eaters up to 20 feet long.

Despite their evolutionary success for more than 50 million years, the amphibians had to spend part of their life cycle in water. Since their eggs lacked a protective covering that would prevent them from drying out on the land, all amphibians had to return to the water to lay their jelly-soft eggs. This continues to be true for modern amphibians, a group that includes salamanders, newts, frogs, and toads. All lay their eggs in water, where they are fertilized. The eggs then develop into tadpoles which complete that stage of their life cycle in water. They then shed their fishlike tails and crawl ashore as adults. Although they were the first vertebrates to colonize the land, the amphibians never became completely adapted for life on the land.

The Carboniferous was a time of swamp formation. In the many swamps of the period, matted organic material was compressed and formed peat, the first stage in coal formation.

Well before the close of the Devonian 345 million years ago, many other animals had taken up life on the land—including millipedes, scorpions, spiders, and the first insects, which lacked wings—but the amphibians were the only vertebrates. Among Devonian plant life on land were horsetail rushes, tall tree ferns with stems more than 3 feet thick, and forests of scale trees reaching heights of nearly 50 feet.

FROM AMPHIBIANS TO REPTILES

During the next geologic period, the Carboniferous, the land changed in important ways. Shallow seas continued to cover much of the Northern Hemisphere early in the period. Extensive mountains were raised in western Europe, and the Ouachita Mountains of Oklahoma and Arkansas were thrust up. One-hundred-foot-high scale trees were common along the edges of pools, shallow lakes, and swamps, and below them was a dense undergrowth of ferns and other plants.

During the later Carboniferous some areas of the land alternately sank, creating large lakes and swamps, then rose above sea level again. Each time, old forests died and new ones took their places. Gradually layer upon layer of matted organic matter was compressed in the water and formed that substance we call peat, the first stage in coal formation. With each lowering of the land, seawaters flowed over the peat, covering it with new sediment deposits that often contained fossil remains. So today we find layers of coal alternating with layers of sedimentary rock. About half of the world's workable coal was formed during the late Carboniferous, mainly from the giant scale trees.

Judging from the number of fossil teeth and fin spines from this period, sharks were abundant in the warm waters of the Carboniferous. There were many terrestrial creatures as well—centipedes and scorpions from earlier times, land snails, and hundreds of species of cockroaches, some big ones 4 inches long. Cockroaches are another example of living fossils, generalists marvelously adapted for survival in a wide range of environments, including modern kitchen cabinets.

But so many amphibians continued to roam the land that the

Carboniferous Period is called the Age of Amphibians. The amphibians remained the only dominant animals with backbones until a newcomer, the reptiles, appeared late in the period and eventually replaced the amphibians both on land and in the seas. Early examples of reptiles about a foot long have been found in sedimentary rock of Nova Scotia. The reptiles inherited a climate and landscape rather different from the one that saw the rise of the amphibians.

This reconstruction of a Pennsylvanian tailed amphibian, "Diplovertebron," shows a stage in amphibian evolution more advanced than the lobe fins of the Devonian. True locomotion overland was made possible by much-improved limbs.

The Permian Period, which lasted nearly as long as the Carboniferous, also was a time for great change. The Appalachians south of New England were thrust up, and the Ural Mountains of Russia were formed. Along the west coast of North America there was widespread volcanic activity. While the western United States was still covered by shallow seas during this period, in other parts of the Northern Hemisphere inland seas were drying up and leaving vast deposits of salt and potash.

Most of the Permian forests were made up of cone-bearing trees like our present-day pines, firs, and spruce. The giant horsetails and scale trees of earlier times became smaller, although ferns, tree ferns, and seed ferns continued to thrive.

A general drying of the land during the Permian is suggested by the huge success of reptiles and a gradual decline in amphibians. Without sufficient water in which to lay their eggs, amphibians could not be expected to thrive. So a significant climate change tipped the scales in favor of reptiles over amphibians.

Two things gave the reptiles a major advantage over the amphibians.

Eryops *was a large amphibian of the Permian. This specimen, found in Texas, was about 6 feet long and lived near water, where it fed mostly on fishes.*

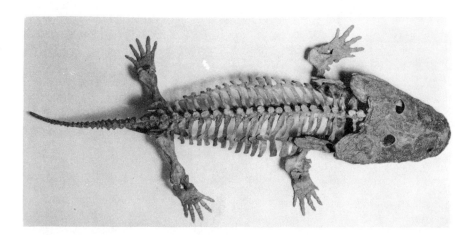

One was a new kind of egg. Remember that amphibian eggs had to be laid in water in order to survive since they lacked a protective coating to prevent them from drying out on land. The eggs of reptiles, on the other hand, had a hard shell that retained the watery fluid inside for the developing young and at the same time let oxygen pass through to fuel the embryo.

The reptilian young were packaged in such a protective way that female reptiles could lay their eggs far inland, away from water and predator amphibians. The reptile egg—called an amniote egg—also contained a large supply of yolk, food for the developing embryo. On hatching from its egg, a newborn reptile was ready to take up life on the land, a miniature version of its parent. Reptiles were the first true land-dwelling vertebrates that no longer had to return to water for part of their lives.

The second thing that gave reptiles an advantage over their amphibian ancestors was a revised body plan. The reptilian jaw was powerful and equipped with bladelike teeth capable of cutting food. Reptiles also evolved a new kind of protein called keratin, which made their skin watertight, and their legs were more efficient, enabling them to outpace their amphibian rivals during the chase or escape.

Marking the changeover from amphibians to reptiles was a type called *Seymouria,* whose fossils have been found in west Texas. While some biologists look on *Seymouria* as an advanced amphibian, others regard it as a primitive reptile. In any case, *Seymouria* clearly bridges the gap between amphibians and reptiles, and quite likely all reptiles evolved from *Seymouria.*

Early in the Permian, some 280 million years ago, a group of finback reptiles, the pelycosaurs, became the ruling meat-eaters. Some lived in swamps and probably spent part of their lives in water. There was the vicious-looking *Dimetrodon* some 11 feet long with sharp teeth capable of ripping apart prey. *Dimetrodon* had skin-covered spines that formed a 5-foot-high fin rising from its back. No one knows for certain what the fin was for, but one educated guess is that it was a means of controlling

Dimetrodon *fin-backs were mammallike reptiles that roamed over what is now Texas in the early Permian. The animals were about 6 feet in length. Their "sails" may have been used to help regulate body temperature.*

body heat, catching heat from the Sun and warming the animal when it was cool, and releasing heat to the air when the animal was too hot.

Most reptiles, by the way, were cold-blooded, like modern snakes and lizards whose body temperatures go up and down with the air or ground temperature. Cold-blooded animals are at a disadvantage since they have to rest frequently to renew the heat lost through exercise, or to avoid overheating in the hot sunlight.

Dimetrodon belonged to a group said to be "mammallike reptiles" because of their skull shape and because mammals evolved from them. By mid-Permian times an especially mammallike group called the therapsids had evolved. Their legs were arranged under them, rather than sticking out from their sides as with modern crocodiles and other reptiles, and their teeth were varied—including fangs for puncturing and molars for chopping and crushing.

Some biologists suspect that the therapsids were warm-blooded, like mammals, meaning that their body chemistry worked to keep the body at a constant temperature. Their warm-bloodedness may not have worked as well as ours does, but it gave the therapsids an important advantage over their cold-blooded relatives. For example, they could be more active in their search for food. Their advanced jaws and limbs also gave them an advantage over the pelycosaurs.

By the late Permian, about 245 million years ago, therapsid groups of many shapes, sizes, and life-styles had become numerous through adaptive radiation, as had the magnificent trilobites during the Cambrian. Meanwhile, the less fit finbacks and all other pelycosaurs had become extinct. By the end of the Permian Period many of the therapsids shared the same fate during the mass extinction that occurred then.

The late Permian was a time of much dying among organisms, especially those living in the shallow seas. Over a span of only a million years, some 90 percent or more of *all* species are thought to have become extinct. Gone were the trilobites, the ancient corals, most brachiopods, crinoids, and bryozoans. The cause of this mass extinction, the greatest known extinction in the history of life on Earth, has long been a major biological mystery. But in recent years geological evidence that the continents have been moving about throughout Earth's history has removed some of the mystery.

Near the end of the Permian, the coming together of the continents greatly reduced the total area of shallow seas. Also, widespread ice sheets covering South America, South and Central Africa, India, Australia, and Antarctica—all joined as Gondwana—withdrew much water from the seas and caused a general lowering of the ocean level. Possibly during late Permian times the sea level lowered enough to expose the continental shelves and so eliminate most of the shallow seas and the many life forms they supported.

The close of the Permian Period, 245 million years ago, marked the end of the Paleozoic Era, or era of "ancient life," and ushered in the Mesozoic Era, or era of "middle life."

CHANGES DURING THE MESOZOIC

Where the Paleozoic Era spanned about 335 million years, the Mesozoic covered only about half that time. But the Mesozoic was a time of great change in life forms, environments, and geography. Including the Triassic, Jurassic, and Cretaceous periods, the Mesozoic is known as the Age of Reptiles for the huge success of these animals. But they were not the old reptiles of the Permian Period. Instead, they were entirely new lines, and they were everywhere. There were about 75 percent more reptiles then than there are now, and they were to rule supreme for some 150 million years. Humans, on the other hand, have been around only a few hundreds of thousands of years, only a fraction of 1 percent of the time organic evolution has been going on.

By about 220 million years ago—during the mid-Triassic—one line of reptiles had evolved into the "terrible lizards," the dinosaurs. The ancestors of the dinosaur giants were lizardlike animals, about the size of a large dog, called thecodonts. Swift, and with excellent vision for spotting prey, the thecodonts also gave rise to flying reptiles, the pterosaurs, and to birds. Fossils of early dinosaurs found in New Mexico belong to a dinosaur group known as lizard-hips (saurischians) because of the way their hips were arranged. The lizard-hips ran about on two muscular hind legs. While some were meat-eaters, others preferred a vegetarian life-style. It was the lizard-hips that evolved into the monsters *Tyrannosaurus rex* and *Allosaurus.*

A second group of Triassic dinosaurs also were to evolve into some of the Jurassic and Cretaceous giants. These were known as the bird-hips (ornithischians). Fossils of early members of this group have been found in Cape Province, South Africa. Unlike the lizard-hips, which typically had powerful hind legs with tiny forelimbs, the bird-hips kept their large forelegs. They browsed in marshes and lagoons and eventually

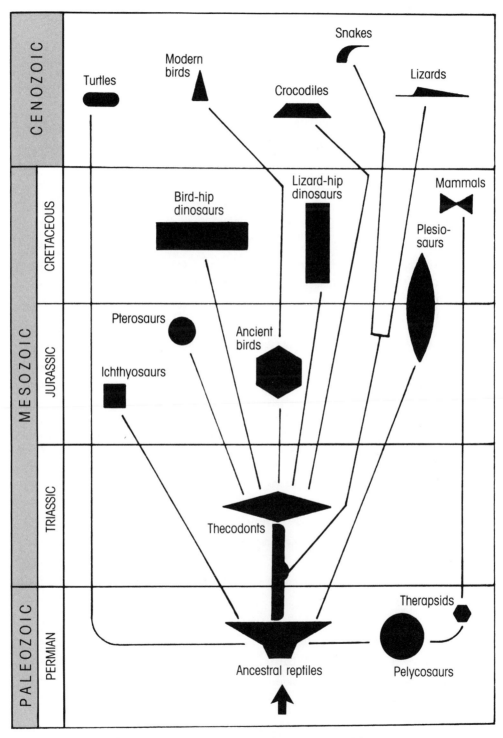

ADAPTIVE RADIATION OF REPTILES

evolved into the water-loving and plant-eating duckbill dinosaurs. Other heavy-legged descendants of the bird-hips were *Stegosaurus* of the Jurassic and *Triceratops* of the Cretaceous.

In 1986 scientists from Columbia University and Harvard University uncovered the largest North American collection of animal fossils from the late Triassic, some 200 million years ago. More than one hundred thousand fossils of skulls, teeth, jaws, and bones from dinosaurs, sharks, lizards, crocodiles, and early fish were discovered. The scientists also found a series of dinosaur footprints, each the size of a penny, the smallest-ever dinosaur remains. As the remains continue to be studied, new knowledge about the ancestors of several present-day animal groups—including crocodiles—should be revealed.

Before the close of the Triassic, 195 million years ago, corals and algae produced extensive limestone deposits that later were thrust up as the Dolomite Alps of northern Italy. In the next period, the Jurassic, pieces of Gondwana and Laurasia broke apart and formed the continental land masses familiar to us today, even though the continents had not yet drifted to their present positions. The climate was generally mild and moist because there were no major land masses at the north or south polar regions to accumulate snow and ice.

The giant sequoias and pine trees so familiar today came into their own late in the Jurassic. Jurassic swamps provided rich vegetation for the plant-eating dinosaurs including *Diplodocus, Brachiosaurus, Cetiosaurus,* and *Apatosaurus,* all weighing 20 tons or more and measuring 60 feet from tail to snout. The ammonites of earlier days, coiled hard-shelled animals the size of silver dollars, became especially plentiful. There were so many of them and they came in such variety that paleontologists have been able to use them to identify and compare rock layers.

REPTILES WHO RETURNED TO THE SEA

Cataloging Jurassic life forms could go on for many pages. It will be more useful, however, to examine some of the evolutionary trends that took place at various times during the three Mesozoic periods. For one, certain land-dwelling reptiles took up life in the water. Among them were the phytosaurs, which evolved from Triassic thecodonts, and the crocodiles. By the way, we can add crocodiles to our growing list of living fossils, since they have changed very little from Jurassic times to the present. But that is not the point of bringing them in here.

Since both Jurassic crocodiles and phytosaurs had evolved on land, both were air-breathers and had lungs. Evolution does not work in reverse, so even though both forms took up life in the water they did not reevolve gills as a means of taking in oxygen any more than they reevolved soft eggs. Because they kept their reptilian land eggs with hard shells, both had to return to the land to lay their eggs, as modern turtles do, a situation opposite to that of the amphibians.

A casual look might lead one to believe that crocodiles evolved from phytosaurs, since the two look so very much alike. But a closer look shows that the crocodiles must have had their own thecodont ancestry and one different from that of the phytosaurs. The telltale difference is in the way they breathe.

The phytosaurs had nostrils high on their foreheads, mounted on snorkellike structures that led down to the back of their mouths. The crocodiles had no such arrangement. Instead, they had bony plates that allowed air from their nostrils to follow a dry passageway along the roof of their mouths. This enabled a crocodile to lie in wait in the water with its mouth submerged and open, waiting for food to swim by. Here were two different solutions to the same problem, evolved by two animal types from different, although closely related, ancestral stock.

Among other reptiles who returned to take up life in the water were the dolphinlike ichthyosaurs and the long-necked plesiosaurs with their short bodies which they moved through the water with large paddle-shaped legs. Rather than returning to the land to lay their eggs, female ichthyosaurs hatched their eggs inside their body.

In no case of reptiles who took to the water was there one in which gills were reinvented. The rule in evolution is that once lost, a structure is never regained.

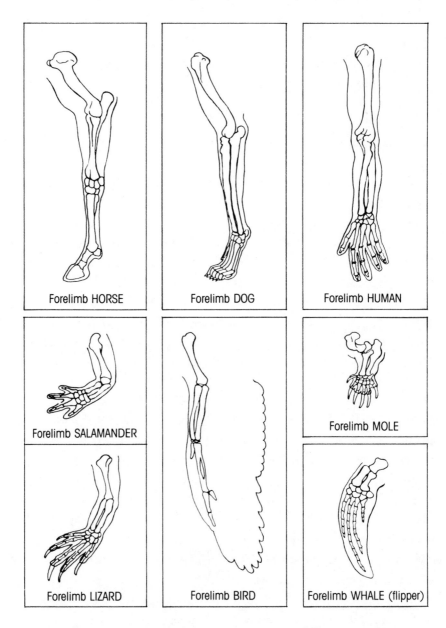

Forelimb HORSE

Forelimb DOG

Forelimb HUMAN

Forelimb SALAMANDER

Forelimb LIZARD

Forelimb BIRD

Forelimb MOLE

Forelimb WHALE (flipper)

"The conclusion is inescapable that the limb bones of man, the bat, and the whale are modifications of a common ancestral pattern. The facts admit of no other logical interpretation. . . . {T}he forelimbs of all tetrapod vertebrates exhibit a unity of anatomical pattern intelligible only on the basis of common inheritance."—E. Peter Volpe, Understanding Evolution *(William C. Brown Company, Publishers)*

REPTILES WHO TOOK TO THE AIR

The first flying reptiles appeared during the Jurassic. They were the pterosaurs, "dragons of the air." Two long bony arms and clawlike fingers attached to a sheet of skin formed wings. These bulky fliers with wing spans up to 50 feet must have needed a long takeoff run to become airborne. They probably dive-bombed for fish from time to time and could walk as well as fly. The pterosaurs also trace their ancestry back to the thecodonts.

As the snout structure for breathing in phytosaurs and crocodiles evolved along different but parallel paths, so did the wings in butterflies, dragonflies, pterosaurs, and birds. Anyone who takes a close look at the plan of a dragonfly wing and compares it with the plan of a chicken wing will find major differences, the chicken wing with its folding bone frame being much more advanced than the boneless dragonfly wing. This is because the two wing types had very different origins in evolution and came from very different ancestors, even though both are limbs evolved for flying.

In a sense the similarity of wings in this instance is false and can be termed an analogue, meaning that although they are similar in function they are not similar in structure and do not have a common origin. But within the line of vertebrates there are similarities in limb design that are true and unmistakably reveal a common ancestry. They are called homologues.

Study the drawings on the facing page and carefully compare the shaded bones of the forelimbs of a horse, dog, human being, salamander, lizard, bird (wing), mole, and whale (flipper). In each instance there are two bones (shaded) called the radius and ulna, although in horses they are fused, and an upper arm bone called the humerus. In each case there are "fingers," although the fingers of horses are fused into a hoof and the fingers of birds evolved a somewhat different shape. Homologues such as these are among the most convincing evidence of common ancestry and, therefore, of the fact of evolution. Evolution is the only logical explanation for the homologous structures that occur in both the animal and plant kingdoms.

10

Descendants of the Reptiles

FROM REPTILES TO BIRDS

If it flies, it isn't necessarily a bird. There are flying fish, flying squirrels, and there were the pterosaur flying reptiles, but none was a bird. True birds evolved from reptiles during the Jurassic, and so successful were these airborne newcomers that before the end of the Jurassic about 90 percent of the bird families alive today had become established.

To date, paleontologists have discovered in Solnhofen limestone deposits in southern Germany five fossils of a reptile-bird known as *Archaeopteryx,* some 150 million years old. *Archaeopteryx* is one of several transitional types that unmistakably show the evolutionary changeover from one animal type into another, in this case from reptiles to birds. Fully clothed in true feathers, instead of scales, and about the size of a crow, *Archaeopteryx* was an agile Cessna of the airways compared with the earlier pterosaur flying boxcar that was better constructed for gliding than for active flying. There can be no doubt about *Archaeopteryx*'s link with reptiles. It had the toothed jaw of a reptile and a reptilian tail.

In 1988 paleontologists digging in the Las Hoyas limestone formation in Cuenca, Spain, uncovered a robin-size fossil about 120 million

Archaeopteryx, *the first known bird from the fossil record, was discovered in southern Germany. About 18 inches long, this 150-million-year-old fossil shows an evolutionary changeover from reptiles to birds.*

years old. It has been identified as a transitional type linking *Archaeopteryx* with later birds.

Evolutionary biologists wish they could find more such transitional types, which have a mixture of primitive and advanced traits, but they are not common. There are enough of them, however, to put away any doubts that transitional types exist, and many more are bound to be discovered.

If evolution were *always* a process of slow and gradual change that needed tens or hundreds of millions of years, we might expect to find more transitional forms in the fossil record. But according to paleontologists Niles Eldredge and Stephen J. Gould, evolution does not *always* proceed that slowly or smoothly. Sometimes it surges ahead, one animal or plant group evolving into quite a different group in only a few million years. Although that may seem a long time, considering the chance of an animal or a plant of a transitional type becoming a fossil, it is a rather short time. The idea that evolution seems to occur in relatively rapid spurts is termed "punctuated equilibria."

This is a good place to come back to the evolutionary business of homologues and parallel evolution, again with the aid of pictures. Vertebrates took to the air at least three separate times during the Mesozoic—as pterosaurs, birds, and bats—and each time with a somewhat different wing design, although each one showed that all three types came from closely related ancestors. The wings of all three have the upper arm bone (humerus)—just as you do—then the two lower arm bones, radius and ulna, then a wrist at the end of which are "fingers." But now notice the differences.

The pterosaur wing had four fingers. Three were in the form of little claws used for grasping while the fourth was stretched out into four longer bones that supported the skin-wing. In birds, which came along next in the evolutionary time scale, the plan is quite different. While birds have the humerus and double bone radius and ulna, they have only three short fingers. Now notice the pattern in bats, which are mammals and which came along later. The humerus, radius, and ulna are there but there is only a single finger-hook. The other four fingers spread out and form a fan support for the skin-covered wing.

In all three cases of pterosaurs, birds, and bats, the forelimbs, which we call "wings," were adapted for flight independently and in somewhat different ways. The differences reflect independent adaptations created by genetic design. But the rather similar basic design is explained by the common ancestry of all three animal types.

FROM REPTILES TO MAMMALS

Like birds, mammals also evolved from reptiles. We can trace our ancestry to those Permian mammallike reptiles, the therapsids, which bridged the gap between reptiles and mammals, as *Archaeopteryx* bridged the gap between reptiles and birds, and as *Seymouria* bridged the gap between

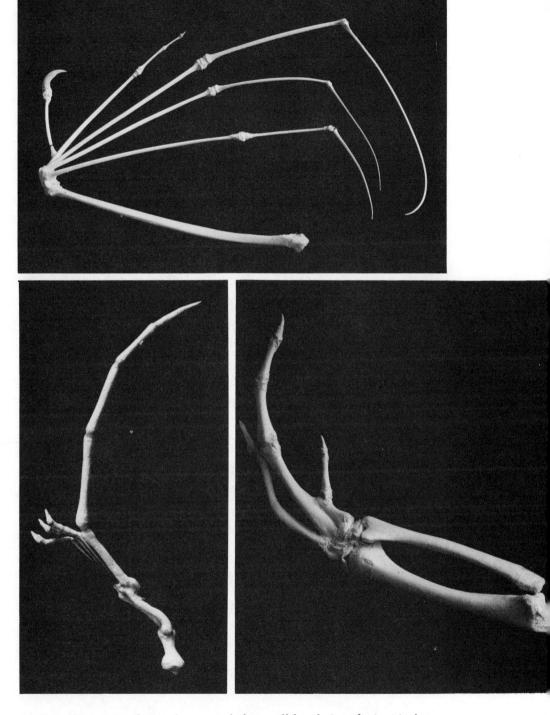

These photographs of wing bones reveal the parallel evolution of wings in bats (top), pterosaurs (lower left), and birds, in this case a hen (lower right).

amphibians and reptiles. By the end of the Triassic true mammals had evolved. Although small, about the size of rats or a small cat, they were important evolutionary newcomers. To qualify as a mammal an animal must have body hair (an adaptation for warmth), give birth to offspring rather than lay eggs, provide milk for its offspring, and be warm-blooded.

Fossils of early Jurassic mammals are rare. We have only a few jaws and bits and pieces of other bones found in China, East Africa, and southern Wales. The early mammals may have been most active in search of insects for food during the cool of the night when the cold-blooded reptiles were sluggish and inactive. Another thing that sets the mammals—and birds—apart from reptiles is that they tend to give birth to fewer young and look after their young until they are able to shift for themselves. Reptiles and amphibians lay many eggs and leave their young to shift for themselves.

As a group, mammals didn't do much for well over 100 million years, except to stay around by managing to keep out of the way of the

The Jurassic was the time the first fossils of true mammals were formed. About the only clues to what these animals were like are several tiny jawbones (top left) that have been found. The animals, which seem to have resembled shrews, were about the size of rats, or close to the size of large dinosaur eggs.

flesh-eating reptiles. It's as if the mammals were waiting for the right moment to expand and take over, and that moment came around the close of the Cretaceous Period, 66 million years ago.

It was during the Cretaceous that the two major modern groups of mammals became established. One group, the placentals, includes most of today's mammals. The name comes from a membrane (the placenta), which separates the mother from its developing embryo and through which the embryo receives nourishment and rids itself of wastes. The other group, the marsupials, includes species of Australia—kangaroos, wombats, koalas—and the North American opossum. In marsupials the young are born at a much earlier stage and transferred to a special pouch where they are protected and have access to milk from the mother. Today's opossums, by the way, are little changed from their Cretaceous ancestors, so they may join our list of living fossils.

The bony fish that swam Cretaceous seas were those we know today. Their small, thin scales, harder skeletons, and sleeker tails and fins replaced the less efficient structures of their Jurassic ancestors.

As mammals were becoming established during this period, so were plant newcomers—the flowering plants. Much of the vegetation found in the old Carboniferous coal-producing areas was replaced by the more efficient flowering plants. The seeds of earlier, non-flowering plants were exposed to the elements and so in danger of being destroyed, whereas flowering plants protected their seeds within hard nuts or encased them in fruits. This evolutionary invention among plants gave the flowering plants an important advantage, and they spread far and wide in water as well as on land.

The distribution of fossil marsupials, and other animal and plant forms, is added evidence for continental drift throughout geologic time. For example, before Gondwana and Laurasia split off from the super-continent Pangaea, reptiles were free to roam from one edge of the world to the other. That is why we find reptilian fossils distributed fairly uniformly over the various large land masses. This was also true of the earliest mammals, but by the time of the explosive evolutionary expansion

Large coiled ammonoids browsed over the floor of Cretaceous shallow seas. There also were many straight-shelled ammonoids. The reconstruction here is based on fossil finds at Coon Creek, Tennessee.

of the mammals, Gondwana and Laurasia had split apart and broken up into, among other lands, those pieces we now call Australia, North America, and South America, all three of which were surrounded by water. The water served as a geographical barrier that kept certain animal and plant groups confined to certain areas. The marsupials of Australia are an example.

In recent years, some geologists have come to think that there probably is a "supercontinent cycle," a time when a single giant land mass is broken up into many smaller continents which then, over millions of years, rejoin once again as another Pangaea. Cause of the continental breakup is heat beneath the supercontinent, which causes the continent to dome upward and break apart. Pangaea may be only the most recent supercontinent to break up during one phase in the supercontinent cycle.

THE GREAT EXTINCTION

The closing of the Cretaceous saw another mass extinction, such as that that had happened in the late Permian. This one wiped out the dinosaurs who had ruled the land for 150 million years. Of the reptiles, only a few made it through to modern times, including lizards, snakes, crocodiles, and turtles. Many other species also bit the dust, but the mammals survived.

The dinosaurs' passing marked the second great dying, and the cause for it has yet to be learned. The debate has been a lively one for many years, and almost every year new evidence and new theories to explain the mass extinction are offered.

The answer has to be found in marked environmental change and the inability of plant and animal species to adapt to the change. But to what part(s) of the environment do we look for a cause, or causes? Could changes in the amount of free oxygen in the atmosphere have taken place? A large increase, or decrease, in free oxygen would put large numbers of plants and animals under great evolutionary stress.

What are some other possible causes for the Cretaceous mass extinction? Could the Sun's energy output have changed temporarily? Could there have been a temporary increase in ultraviolet radiation, or of deadly cosmic rays? Some scientists say that every 50 million years Earth's magnetic field weakens and so permits a massive inflow of cosmic rays. The next tidal wave of cosmic rays, they say, may sweep over the planet in A.D. 4000. Or could sudden climate change have been the cause?

Some scientists think that one or more large comets or asteroids smashed into the planet. Luis Alvarez, a physicist at the University of California at Berkeley, launched this controversial idea around 1979. The resulting explosive impact from a large comet or asteroid could have raised a massive cloud of dust that would have been blown high into the air and carried around the globe. Such a cloud might hang in the air for a year, blocking out large amounts of the Sun's energy and bringing about rapid cooling, a climate change that would have spelled doom to many species, including the dinosaurs.

The British geologist Anthony Hallam thinks that increased volcanic activity over a long period might have caused serious ecosystem collapse. He says that widespread lava flows would have released destructive amounts of sulfur into the lower atmosphere, resulting in acid rain that could have destroyed marine and land ecosystems alike.

A number of other scientists, Eldredge among them, also feel that the Cretaceous extinction was not a sudden affair, that it had begun millions of years earlier and then somehow speeded up during the late Cretaceous. S. M. Stanley of Johns Hopkins University has said that a comet impact late in the Cretaceous would have made an already bad situation truly awful. Says Eldredge, "We really are dealing with the [slow] collapse of ecosystems here." Recent evidence for such a gradual start has come from William Zinsmeister of Purdue University who has studied Cretaceous extinction patterns on Seymour Island, near the Antarctic peninsula. "In high latitudes, you just don't see the marked extinctions. . . . [Instead] you see a gradual change, a gradual dropoff," he said.

We must remember that geological history has seen many mass extinctions—at the end of the Cambrian, during the upper Devonian, at the end of the Permian, in the final years of the Triassic, and then again in the late Cretaceous. And each time, evolution was given a new opportunity to surge ahead.

Whatever the cause(s) of the Cretaceous mass extinction—and the argument may never be settled—gone were the dinosaurs and many other animal groups. The result was another opening up of ecosystems. The news was out and evolution responded. Here was just the condition the mammals had been waiting for for 150 million years. The mass extinction marked the close of the Cretaceous Period and the start of the modern era of the Cenozoic.

NEW TRENDS IN THE CENOZOIC

As the reptiles before them had exploded into many new species through adaptive radiation on the death of the amphibians, so did the mammals invade all the new ecological nooks and crannies left vacant by the Cretaceous extinction of those masses of reptilian forms. This theme has become common in the story of evolution: Environmental change kills off large numbers of species of one group of animals or plants and at the same time provides new opportunities for other groups to repopulate the land through adaptive radiation. This was especially so with the mammals, which had their beginnings as the "rats" of the Mesozoic but by the beginning of the Cenozoic had evolved new forms of many shapes, sizes, and behaviors.

Complexity is a word we should keep in mind as we trace the advance of evolution through the Cenozoic, for life became more complex as it took advantage of every ecological opportunity to fill all available corners of the environment. Darwin observed that fact as a young man when he was in South America. In later years he was to recall: "We may well affirm that every part of the world is habitable! Whether lakes of brine, or those underground ones hidden beneath volcanic mountains, or warm mineral springs, or the wide expanse and depths of the ocean, or the upper regions of the atmosphere, and even the surface of perpetual snow— all support living things."

The Cenozoic Era, meaning "recent life," began 66 million years ago and brings us to the present. As we cross over into the Cenozoic, known as the Age of Mammals, we will be surveying life and its evolution through time spans called epochs, which are shorter than periods.

EPOCH	MILLIONS OF YEARS AGO	PERIOD
Paleocene	66 to 54	Tertiary
Eocene	54 to 38	Tertiary
Oligocene	38 to 26	Tertiary
Miocene	26 to 7	Tertiary
Pliocene	7 to 2	Tertiary
Pleistocene	2 to 0.1	Quaternary
Recent	0.1 to now	Quaternary

Most of the modern groups of mammals began to show up in the Eocene Epoch, by which time many older forms had disappeared. Some of the modern forms took up life in the sea (whales and seals), while others took to the air (bats). Recall that the same thing had happened among the reptiles, with plesiosaurs taking up life in the water and pterosaurs taking to the air.

One of the major events of the Paleocene was the evolution of grasses, which by the Miocene had become continuously growing plants able to support large herds of grazing animals. During most of the Cenozoic the western United States saw lots of volcanic activity. Mounts Shasta and Rainier were formed. During much of the era, there was a general rising of the continents, which drained off large areas of inland seas and brought about conditions favorable to widespread grasslands. At one stage a land bridge was thrust up that linked South America with North America and permitted a two-way migration of various animal groups. Before this land link formed, South America had seen the evolution of mammals found nowhere else, as had Australia with its marsupials. There were

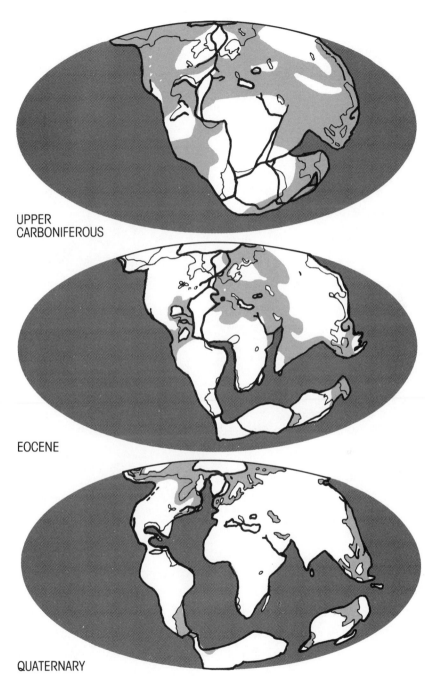

UPPER
CARBONIFEROUS

EOCENE

QUATERNARY

By the beginning of the Cenozoic Era, some 66 million years ago, the continents had drifted apart enough so that we can begin to distinguish their shapes, although North America and Europe were still joined, as were Antarctica and Australia.

Among the many giant mammals of the last ice age that covered much of North America were four species of mammoths, which probably migrated from Siberia some 2 million years ago. The largest ones stood 13 feet high at the shoulders, weighed 6 to 8 tons, and had tusks up to 11 feet long. About 1,500 mammoth sites have been found in North America.

giant sloths and several groups of grazing animals, fossils of which have been found only in South America.

The great age of mammals peaked before the Pleistocene some 2 million years ago. Among the many giant forms that roamed the land then were woolly mammoths and mastodons, 18-foot-high ground sloths, long-horned bison, and 7-foot-long beavers. But by the end of the last ice age, some 10,000 years ago, all of them were gone, along with North

America's elephants, camels, horses, dire wolves, and saber-toothed cats. What caused this most recent wave of extinction?

A series of major climate changes took place during the Cenozoic. The drifting of Antarctica to its present position at the South Pole provided a large land mass capable of accumulating vast amounts of ice and snow, which led to a general lowering of sea level and the drying up of many inland seas. There have been several ice ages since then, and Antarctica has been under a deep crust of ice for the past 4 to 5 million years.

Large animals seem to be better able to withstand a cold climate, since they lose body heat less rapidly than small animals do. But the environmental tables turned at the end of the last ice age, when the great sheets of ice withdrew and with them many of the spruce-forest habitats favored by the mastodons, for example. Invading pine and hardwood forests, and grasslands, then took over and favored new groups of animals.

With the great melt that ended the last ice age 10,000 years ago, the land emerged as the land we know today, with all of its familiar plants and animals in place, including human beings who by then had been around for a long time. To trace the evolution of those early mammals that gave rise to human beings, we must turn the geological clock back to the beginning of the Cenozoic Era.

It is not because Darwin concluded that evolution has occurred that scientists believe it, but because he discovered the evidence from which they can see for themselves that it has.

—Sir Gavin de Beer, 1964

11

Human Evolution

PRIMATES MAKE THEIR BID

An important, for us, event began to change the world near the beginning of the Cenozoic, some 70 million years ago. Around that time the small, ratlike, insect-eating mammals underwent adaptive radiation and branched out into two dozen or more different groups. Among them is a group called primates. The primates in turn split off into three groups, one of which eventually gave rise to human beings.

One of those primate groups consists of tree shrews. Another includes the prosimians—today's lemurs and tarsiers. Some prosimians are about the size of a squirrel. The smallest is the gray mouse lemur, which weighs only 2 ounces. Most are active at night, as were the early mammals. All have forward-facing eyes, an adaptation for depth vision, and handlike limbs adapted for grasping and making their way through the trees where they spend their lives. The prosimians living in the wild today are found only in Madagascar, Africa, Asia, and Southeast Asia. The third branch of the primate group is the hominoid branch, which includes apes and human beings.

The members of all three primate groups took to the trees as a way of life. By doing so they avoided competition with other mammals who remained on the ground, and they found a place safe from predators. To live successfully in the trees required two important adaptations: 1) the evolution of "fingers" and toes with claws (which later became nails in human beings) capable of grasping tree branches; and 2) forward-facing eyes, instead of eyes at the sides of the head. Forward-facing eyes provided much-needed depth perception for life in the trees and for spotting food, which consisted of fruit and insects. There can be no doubt that those, and other, adaptations occurred among the primates early in the Cenozoic, but their history is blurred.

In 1965 paleontologists digging in Montana uncovered the oldest known primate fossil, some 65 million years old. By 10 million years later many primates, up to the size of a modern house cat, lived in North America. Then by 20 million years after that—the early Oligocene—most of these North American primates were gone. Where did they go, and why? Possibly a change to a cooler and drier climate caused most of the North American primates to migrate south to warmer areas. In any case, Africa, not North America, was the scene of the primates' rapid evolution into the hominoid branch.

By this time the prosimians and hominoids had gone their separate ways. We now enter a time when we begin to find very convincing evidence of our evolutionary connection with the remote past. The hominoids' oldest known ancestor to date seems to be an apelike animal weighing about 12 pounds that lived in Egypt some 30 million years ago during the Oligocene. Fittingly, it was given the Latin name *Aegyptopithecus*.

A more recent arrival on the evolutionary scene was another apelike animal called *Dryopithecus,* which evolved some 25 million years ago and stayed around for 15 million years. Its fossil remains have been found in Africa, Europe, and Asia. It seems to be still another transitional form, one which spent part of its time in the trees and part walking about on the ground. Paleontologist Louis Leakey found fossil remains

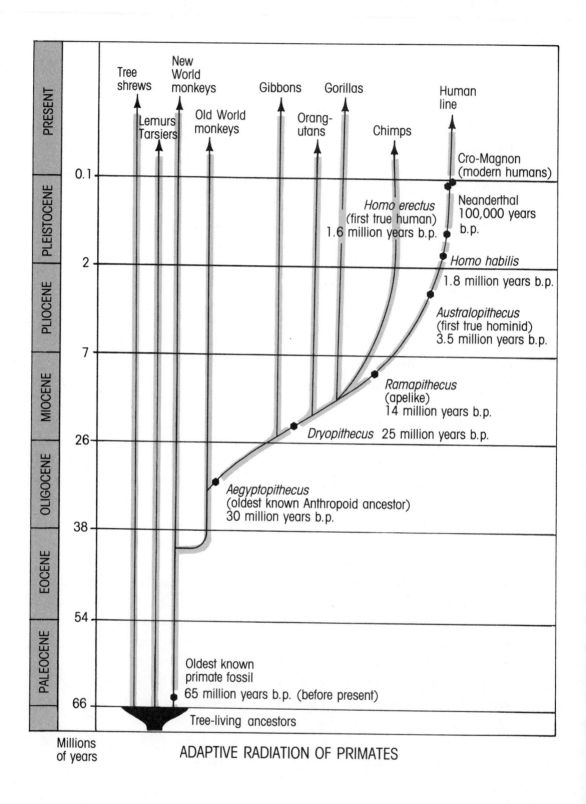

ADAPTIVE RADIATION OF PRIMATES

Millions of years

PRESENT

Tree shrews

Lemurs Tarsiers

New World monkeys

Old World monkeys

Gibbons

Orang-utans

Gorillas

Chimps

Human line

0.1

PLEISTOCENE

Cro-Magnon (modern humans)

Homo erectus (first true human) 1.6 million years b.p.

Neanderthal 100,000 years b.p.

2

Homo habilis 1.8 million years b.p.

PLIOCENE

Australopithecus (first true hominid) 3.5 million years b.p.

7

MIOCENE

Ramapithecus (apelike) 14 million years b.p.

26

Dryopithecus 25 million years b.p.

OLIGOCENE

Aegyptopithecus (oldest known Anthropoid ancestor) 30 million years b.p.

38

EOCENE

54

PALEOCENE

Oldest known primate fossil 65 million years b.p. (before present)

66

Tree-living ancestors

of *Dryopithecus* in Kenya, Africa, in the 1930s. To date, more have been uncovered in China, Egypt, France, Germany, Greece, Hungary, and other places. Some members of *Dryopithecus* were gorilla-size, others the size of a gibbon.

In the 1960s, Leakey and his wife Mary discovered the upper jaw of a skull with teeth having characteristics of human teeth. That is, the teeth formed a curved row and consisted of four types: incisors, canines, premolars, and molars. The skull, found in Kenya, was 14 million years old. This creature was apelike in some ways and manlike in others; it was assigned to the genus *Ramapithecus*. It belonged to a widespread group that lived in Africa, Asia, Greece, Turkey, and Hungary from late Miocene to early Pliocene times. Leakey's *Ramapithecus* skull turned out to match similar bones found in India by G. Edward Lewis in 1935. While some experts regard *Ramapithecus* as an advanced ape, others think of it as a primitive human.

About this time during the late Cenozoic the hominoids in Africa underwent rapid adaptive radiation. Paleontologists suspect that the cause, as in the past, was the opening up of many new ecosystems. During the late Cenozoic, geologic upheaval split East Africa apart, forming the East Africa Rift Valley, a 3,000-mile-long rupture in the crustal rock. Many new environmental nooks and crannies appeared. There were desert environments, lake and tropical forest environments, river environments, and swamp and open plains areas, all displaying evolutionary for-rent signs, and evolution was ready to fill them with new species.

Facing page: *The primates evolved from tree-living ancestors and, according to one interpretation, gave rise to three major groups: tree shrews, prosimians (lemurs and tarsiers), and anthropoids (monkeys, apes, and humans). As new fossil finds are made and analyzed, the primate family tree continues to change with the addition of relatively new members such as* Homo habilis *and* Aegyptopithecus. *Each new primate fossil find is an exciting event since it reveals more about our human ancestry.*

RISE OF THE HOMINOIDS

Adaptive radiation of the hominoids gave rise to several new apelike forms. There were chimpanzees, which became associated with seasonally changing wet and dry climates. Another new group, gorillas, became associated with the ever-warm and humid tropical forests. And in regions of increasing dryness we find sound evidence of still another newcomer, the first true hominids, which may be more than 5 million years old, although no fossils of that age have yet turned up.

Many fossils of this humanlike group, called *Australopithecus,* meaning "southern ape-man," keep turning up in Africa. The first was identified in South Africa by the anatomist Raymond Dart in 1924. It was the skull of a six-year-old child with distinctly human teeth. The oldest *Australopithecus* fossil remains found to date are about 3.5 million years old and were uncovered in Hadar, Ethiopia, in 1974 by anthropologists Donald C. Johanson of the Cleveland Museum and Tim D. White of the University of California at Berkeley. Named "Lucy" by their discoverers, the bones were of a female who stood about 3 feet 8 inches tall. In 1986 the same researchers found a skull and limb bones of a descendant of Lucy, about 1.8 million years old, while digging in Olduvai Gorge, Tanzania, Africa. The bones were those of a female about thirty years old, who stood about 3 feet tall. Members of her species are called *Homo habilis.*

It is theorized that *Homo habilis* had learned to fashion crude tools out of pebbles, and that they supplemented their vegetable diet with meat. They lived in regions from Africa to Asia and in a short 200,000 years (1.6 million years ago) gave rise to the earliest known distinctly human line, called *Homo erectus,* meaning "upright man." The interesting thing here is the rapid evolutionary change that took place in those 200,000 years. Evolution of the human line moved abruptly from a species only 3 feet tall (*Homo habilis*) to one nearly our size (*Homo erectus*). Here is another example of evolution moving in rapid spurts, according to Eldredge and Gould's idea of punctuated equilibria.

The establishment of *Homo erectus* on the evolutionary landscape

Anthropologist Donald C. Johanson with the reconstructed skull of "Lucy," the oldest Australopithecus *remains yet found, dated at 3.5 million years before present.*

brings us well into the Pleistocene, a time when massive glaciers crept overland and covered large areas of North America and Europe.

Although they were well on the way to becoming modern human beings, *Homo erectus* still had telltale apelike features: powerful jaws, a large face, and a prominent brow bone. But apes they were not. They probably wore animal pelts for warmth against the cold and knew how to make fire and to fashion weapons and stone tools. Their brain size also became larger, and their intelligence probably increased enough to give them some power of speech.

In 1891 Eugene Dubois made the first fossil find of *Homo erectus* descendants. It is known as Java Man. In the 1920s a researcher named Davidson Black made another valuable find in China. A cave used by *Homo erectus* descendants for some 70,000 years revealed that these people were hunters. Among remains found in the cave were cooking hearths, tools, and many bones of the hunters themselves. Some of the bones included cracked-open skulls, suggesting that the hunters may have developed an appetite for human brains. A more likely possibility is that the skulls became cracked under the pressure of burial over thousands of years. These people are called Peking Man. Similar fossil finds in Germany are known as Heidelberg Man. All represent about the same stage in human evolution.

The treasured bones of Peking Man, by the way, mysteriously disappeared from their storage place in China sometime during World War II and have never been recovered. The history and mystery of the bones is fascinatingly recounted in a book listed on page 179 of this book.

Is it possible that here we have the beginning of the modern races of human beings, and that all evolved from the single widespread species *Homo erectus*? Eastern variants could have begun with Java Man and Peking Man while western populations could be represented by variants resembling Heidelberg Man.

HOMO SAPIENS *TAKES OVER*

The next major event in our story of evolution is the beginning of the takeover by modern people. The time is some 300,000 years ago, during the last half of the Pleistocene. By that time the last *Homo erectus* types had disappeared, and there were human populations living in Africa and Asia differing little in appearance from populations living in those regions today. But if we met people of those Pleistocene populations we would notice some differences. They had jaws larger than ours, a slightly longer head, and a somewhat larger face. Because they were so much like us, we call them by our own scientific name *Homo sapiens,* which means "wise man."

The remains of four *Homo sapiens* types between 300,000 and 200,000 years old have been studied, two from France, one from England, and one from Germany. Major differences in jaw size, ruggedness of body, and brain case size divided these populations. Had they remained isolated, separated by some geological barrier, eventually they might have evolved into separate species. But instead, there was mingling and interbreeding among certain populations. During that period a reduction

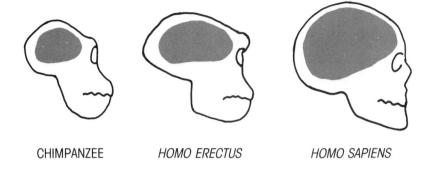

CHIMPANZEE   *HOMO ERECTUS*   *HOMO SAPIENS*

Intelligence and learning are directly related to brain size. Notice in the drawings the changing relationship of brain size to face size from chimps to Homo erectus *to* Homo sapiens. *The skull shown below, exhibiting a large and compactly folded brain, belongs to* Homo sapiens.

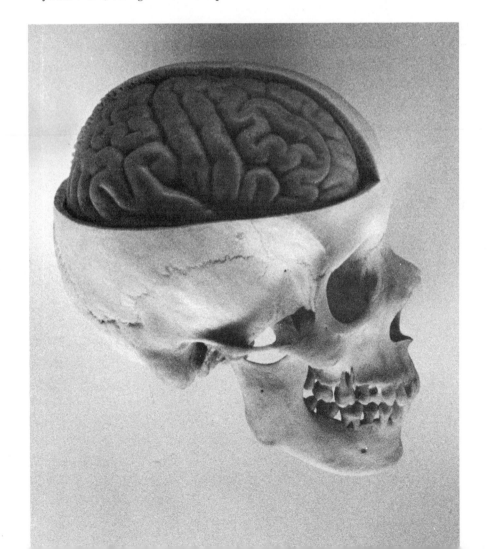

of jaw size to that of modern people occurred among some groups.

The picture of how human beings evolved over the next 200,000 years is still hazy and much debated among anthropologists, although the paleontologist's spade continues to produce new evidence year by year. One group of anthropologists thinks that all modern human beings have as ancestors a population that lived in Africa about 200,000 years ago. Over the next 100,000 years members of that population migrated to other regions, including Europe. As they settled in new regions they replaced existing populations of other, but less able, human types.

Dr. Milford Wolpoff of the University of Michigan says that after *Homo erectus* had spread over the world, modern humans of present-day types then began to evolve. "[M]odern Africans originated in Africa, modern Chinese in eastern Asia, modern Europeans in Europe. And this happened to some extent because all these populations were interconnected by a flow of genes. People were coming and going, exchanging wives, and so on. We think all humanity was interconnected this way. Everywhere you get bigger brains, smaller teeth, all the peculiarities of modern people. How does this happen if there's not an exchange of genes all through human evolution?"

By 115,000 years ago there seem to have been populations of people in southern Africa "totally modern in all observable respects, including the presence of a strongly developed chin," says University of Chicago anthropologist Richard Klein. The major South African site is Klasies River Mouth cave. Klein has worked at four additional South African sites that have yielded human fossils suggesting that modern human beings are at least 100,000 years old. Human fossil evidence found in a cave (Qafzeh) in Israel suggests that modern humans were living there around 92,000 years ago.

Among those relatively "less able" human types who seem to have been overcome by those early modern humans were many populations of large-jawed people who lived in Europe from about 100,000 to 35,000 years. Groups of them also lived in the Near East, and still other groups lived in southwest Asia until about 60,000 years ago. They are known as Neanderthal, and because they are so much like us they share our species name as the subspecies *Homo sapiens neanderthalensis.* Our full species name is *Homo sapiens sapiens.*

THE RISE AND FALL OF NEANDERTHAL

In 1856 fossils of Neanderthal Man were unearthed in a limestone cave in the Neander ravine near Dusseldorf, Germany. These people lived in caves, as well as in the open in tents made of animal skins. Many of the tools they left behind indicate that they were hunters and depended on the meat of Ice Age animals for food and on their skin for clothing and shelter. The Neanderthal brain case was a bit larger than ours, they stood about five feet tall and had powerfully built bodies with big bones. Most likely a descendant of *Homo erectus,* Neanderthal became extinct about 35,000 years ago.

The mystery of Neanderthal's sudden disappearance, after having been around for some 65,000 years, has yet to be solved, but there are theories. Bone digs suggest that over a period of about 5,000 years there was an overlapping of population territories between the large-jawed Neanderthals in Europe and their small-jawed neighbors who lived in the area of Israel and northern Iraq. These small-jawed types were nearly identical to us. Dress one of them in a jogging costume and you wouldn't notice a difference.

One theory had it that the two populations interbred in the zone of overlap and so produced a gene pool that resulted in offspring of both the large-jaw and small-jaw types along with several other anatomical variations. But recent studies of Neanderthal anatomy suggest that there were enough differences between Neanderthals and their small-chin neighbors to have prevented the Neanderthals from evolving into modern humans. Furthermore, the fact that Neanderthals and modern humans lived side by side and preserved their distinct identities for so long makes it unlikely that the two types ever merged, biologically or culturally.

Could cultural and social advances among Neanderthal's modern neighbors have influenced Neanderthal's decline and eventual extinction?

Some 35,000 years ago there seems to have been a burst of such cultural and social activity, as evidenced by prehistoric art discovered in numerous caves in Spain and France. The cave paintings are of bison and other animals of the hunt, and their purpose seems to have been mystical, as if painting an image of the animal before a hunt would somehow bring the hunters good luck. Ritual seems to have played an important role in the lives of the small-jawed populations of this time.

According to Ezra Zubrow, of the State University of New York at Buffalo, "Although Neanderthals were relatively sophisticated in many ways—for instance, they survived huge climate changes, they manufactured an extensive stone tool technology, and they buried their dead—modern humans outstripped them at every step." The Neanderthals may have been looked on as barbarians and been gradually and deliberately killed off by their culturally superior neighbors beginning about 50,000 years ago.

Although there is no evidence for such planned genocide, by about 35,000 years ago all of the Neanderthals were gone. In their place, and populating Europe, Asia, and many other areas of the world, were large groups of small-jawed people just like us, called Cro-Magnon (meaning modern man) or *Homo sapiens sapiens*. Most of the world's human populations have interbred since Cro-Magnon became permanently established, but some may still retain certain characteristics of the Cro-Magnon artists who left their cave paintings for future generations to interpret and admire. Among such groups are the Basque people of northeastern Spain and the Berbers of the Atlas Mountains in North Africa.

One of the liveliest topics in anthropology today is the evolution of modern humans. Another is when the peopling of the Americas took place. About 10,000 years ago the most recent ice sheets withdrew from North America and gave way to the sprawling grasslands of the West. Some 2,000 years earlier, before the ice withdrew, groups of people from Siberia in northern Asia had crossed over to what is now Alaska. They were the Paleo-Indians. In only a few centuries they had evolved rich cultural traditions in settlements ranging from Alaska to the southern tip of South America, and from the Pacific Northwest to Maine and Canada and south to Florida.

Some paleontologists, including several associated with the Center for the Study of Early Man, of the University of Maine at Orono, think that the waves of Paleo-Indian migrations began much earlier, probably at least 30,000 years ago. According to the center's director, Robson Bonnichsen, "for evidence we have the following: flaked mammoth bone dated greater than 30,000 years old from sites in the Old Crow Basin of the northern Yukon Territory; altered bones from El Cedral, northern Mexico more than 33,000 years old, and a long sequence of simple flaked tools from Toca do Boqueirao da Pedra Furada, Brazil, extending back to 31,500 years ago."

THE ORIGIN OF HUMAN RACES

Of all the hominid species, the only one that survived the many snares of evolutionary, cultural, and technological competition is *Homo sapiens*. There are no other human species, although there are various geographical races of *Homo sapiens*.

A "race" within any species can be thought of as a group of populations that have certain physical and genetic characteristics in common and that set that group of populations apart from all other populations of the same species. As Cro-Magnon people increased their numbers and populated virtually every part of the world by about 50,000 years ago, their various populations gradually adapted to various regional environments and so evolved geographical races.

As you have found in earlier chapters in this book, populations of all organisms ebb and flow and change in response to changes in the environment, and they have done so throughout the history of life on this planet. Human populations are no exception, since our genes are subject to environmental pressure just as are the genes of other species. So human populations living in markedly different environments have adapted differently. For example, the Eskimos' relatively short fingers are thought to be an adaptation to a cold environment. Short fingers have less surface area from which to lose heat than do long fingers, so short fingers tend to lessen the risk of frostbite. On the other hand, people adapted to a hot climate tend to have long limbs, an adaptation that promotes heat loss and so prevents overheating of the body. Inhabitants of the Andes mountains of South America have evolved relatively large chests with larger lungs and a larger supply of blood than people living at sea level have. These features are adaptations to life at high altitude, where oxygen is harder to come by because of the lower atmospheric pressure.

The dark skin of the Negroid race may be an adaptation to protect the skin from the damaging action of ultraviolet radiation, which is more intense near the Equator than in middle and high latitudes. So in that environment natural selection might have favored those individuals with the ability to produce lots of melanin, the pigment that darkens the skin. In medium and high latitudes where there is relatively less sunlight, a dark skin can be disadvantageous, since an excess of melanin interferes with vitamin D production in the skin through the action of sunlight. So natural selection at those latitudes might have favored individuals with relatively light skin color.

It is hard to pin down the origin and selective advantage (or disadvantage) of certain variations that have been used to establish the races. Furthermore, such variations are characteristic of *populations*, not of *individuals*. Because that is so, there will always be individuals who cannot be pigeonholed into the racial categories identified with the biologists Franz Weidenerich and Carleton Coon.

Those researchers supposed that the modern races of humans descended from old hominid lines that evolved independently into various racial groups: A Middle East type, perhaps Mount Carmel Man, supposedly led to the Caucasoid (white-skinned) race; Rhodesian Man to the Negroid (black-skinned) race; Peking Man to the Mongoloid (high cheekbones and yellow skin color) race; and Java Man to the Australoid (brown-skinned) race. Still another suggested racial category was the Amerinds (red-skins). So at one stage in hominid history, according to the

Weidenerich-Coon plan, there were a number of pure races that over the centuries became increasingly diluted because of migration and intermixing.

You sometimes hear people speak of the Italian "race" or the Jewish "race." There is, of course, no such thing. There is a Jewish religion or a Catholic religion, people of Italian nationality or French nationality, but none of these makes up a *race*. You also sometimes hear of the Aryan "race," which is another mistaken idea. Aryans are people who speak languages that are offshoots of the root language Indo-European. Such languages include German, Italian, French, English, and others. So anyone who speaks one of those languages as a native is an Aryan. All such people belong to different cultures, not different races.

The idea that the modern human geographical races have evolved as a result of population adaptations over thousands of years is hard to challenge, even if some of the causes are not clear. When different populations of the same species go slightly but significantly separate ways in response to different environmental conditions, we call it parallel evolution. But those separate ways have never led to a fixed and unchanging human race.

There is no such thing as a "pure" race, meaning one that forever remains the same. Because all human beings belong to the same species, our various populations are capable of interbreeding, and interbreeding has been the rule throughout human history. Time and again, as invaders of one geographical race have conquered a neighboring people, the populations have mixed and their racial distinctions have blurred slightly. According to the evolutionary biologist E. Peter Volpe, "The distinguishing features of the basic racial groups have become increasingly blurred by the countless migrations and intermixings. The whole world today is a single large neighborhood. Modern man lives in one great reproductive community."

Races, then, are nothing more than temporary collections of genes in a population's gene pool, temporary and passing stages in the fleeting evolutionary history of a species.

Milestones on the Way to Becoming Human

What were some of the conditions that directed the evolution of human beings along the hominoid line?

WALKING UPRIGHT   The change from a four-footed apelike stance to a two-legged upright posture, beginning around the time of *Dryopithecus* some 25 million years ago, was a major one. It depended on a number of mutations that changed the bone arrangement of the foot and the pelvis. The foot had to be able to take the entire weight of the body, one foot at a time. The pelvis had to change in response to the new angle of the legs.

HANDS   An upright posture meant that the hands were freed for other tasks. Mutations changed the hominid hand and made it much more able than that of the ape and monkey to pick up objects and turn

The human foot evolved in a way that permitted an upright posture. A larger heel and stronger foot arch enable humans to walk upright and flat-footed. Weaker arch bones and smaller heels cause the apes to walk on the outer sides of their feet. Notice the wide gap between the big toe and the rest of the foot in the three primates on the right. These handlike feet do the special job of grasping that is needed for life in the trees.

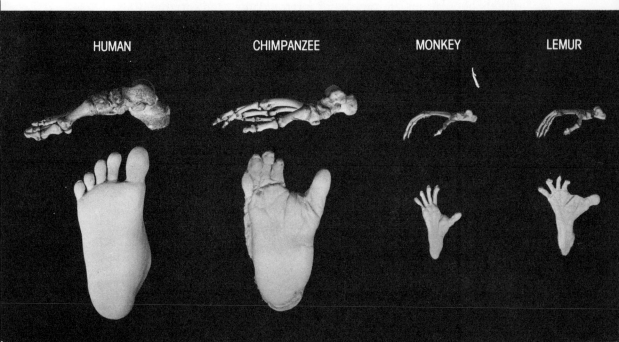

HUMAN   CHIMPANZEE   MONKEY   LEMUR

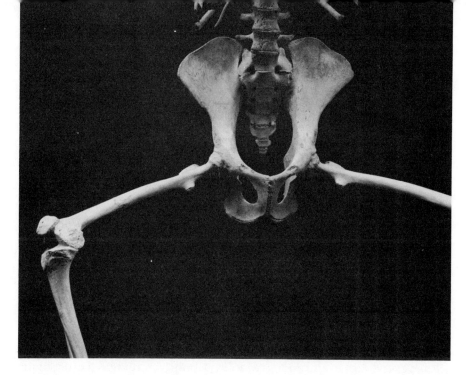

Before the human line could diverge from its apelike ancestor and evolve an upright posture for walking entirely on two legs, an important change in the shape of the pelvis had to occur. Notice the relatively large pelvic bones in the orangutan (above), which permits a stronger arrangement of pelvic and leg muscles for leaping. An upright posture (below) meant a change in the angle of the legs to the broad bones of the pelvis, and an accompanying change in muscle arrangement and gait.

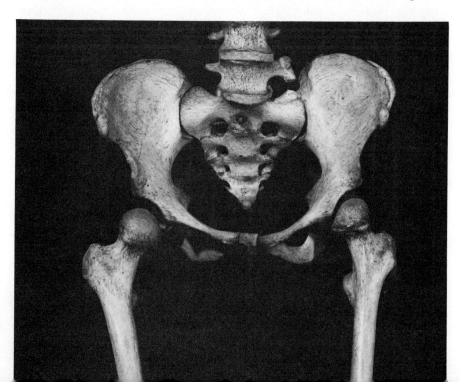

them this way and that for use and examination. The difference between life and death could depend on a weapon held at the ready, or a spear skillfully fashioned and flung at prey.

TOOL USING AND MAKING   Hominids some 2.6 million years ago had learned to use pebbles and stones as hammers and weapons to be flung. And they had learned to improve the shape of a stone to make it a better tool. Although chimps and baboons collect and use sticks of different sizes to dig termites out of crevices or to threaten an enemy, man appears to be the only animal who learned to fashion tools.

THE BRAIN AND INTELLIGENCE   Fine toolmaking required more intelligence—and, therefore, a keener brain—than did simple tool using. Intelligence and learning are directly related to brain size and improvement, and the farther along the line of evolution to *Homo sapiens* we look, the larger and more complex a brain we find. A better brain also meant the ability to develop a complex language and speech. Although chimps and other primates have languages, they are far more limited than human language. A chimp can utter a distress or warning cry that is understood by other chimps, but a chimp never speaks of an out-of-sight predator he would like to get even with. Unlike other primates, people can talk of what happened yesterday or what may happen tomorrow. Even though our gift of language is genetically programmed into us—as are the "languages" of other species—we have to *learn* individual languages. Furthermore, our personal use of language varies greatly and depends on our personal intelligence and education.

TEETH AND DIET   Some 14 million years ago, beginning with *Ramapithecus,* our modern arrangement of teeth that form a curved row had come about. By then, there were also four well-established kinds of teeth: the incisors (used for cutting), the canines (for grasping and tearing), and the premolars and molars (for crushing and grinding). Our tooth structure has changed little since the time of *Homo erectus* some 700,000 years ago, which probably means that diet has changed little since that time also. *Homo erectus* ate plants and meat, just as we do today. They also cooked their food.

TREE SHREW   LEMUR   TARSIER   MONKEY   CHIMPANZEE   HUMAN

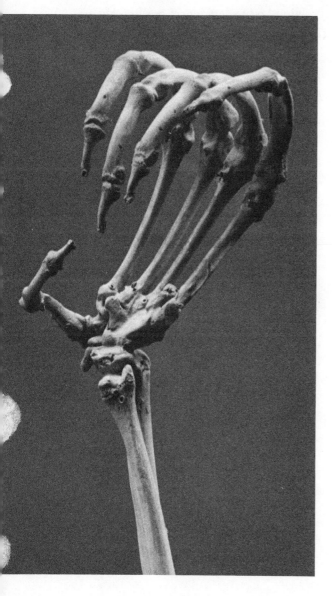

Similarity in structure among related groups of animals (here, the primates) is convincing evidence that they all evolved from a common ancestor. Long claws in tree shrews evolved into nails in monkeys, apes, and humans. Notice the large finger pads of lemurs and tarsiers. The hands of all six primates are specialized for grasping, as clearly shown in the photograph of the hand of an orangutan, a great ape.

That human beings have evolved from earlier hominid groups, which in turn evolved from common ancestors going back some 30 million years, is hard to deny. Our convincing evidence is the fossil record. What is less clear are the exact routes that human evolution has followed over the past few scores of millions of years. But each year, as new fossil finds add to the ever-growing body of evidence, our knowledge of our evolutionary past is enriched and our view of that fascinating past is brought into sharper focus.

I have no doubt that in reality the future will be vastly more surprising than anything I can imagine. Now my own suspicion is that the universe is not only queerer than we suppose, but queerer than we can suppose.

—*John Haldane, 1927*

12

Cultural Evolution and the Future

POPULATIONS AND CULTURE

Today there are thousands of human populations, some adapted to life in the desert, others to life in the tropics, the mountains, or climates of ice and snow. An environmental nook, especially one of climate extremes, sometimes acts as a geographical fence that keeps a given population pretty much to itself and so tends to limit the population's gene pool (people of the Andes, Greenland Eskimos, desert dwellers of the Kalahari, for example).

Cultural forces also tend to isolate certain small, local populations and keep their gene pools limited. Many religious sects in various parts of the world discourage marriage outside their group. The Dunkers, mentioned in Chapter Seven, are one. Segregation by race or social class also is practiced in various parts of the world. In India, where people are divided into social castes, the lowest caste goes by the name of the "untouchables." In New York City and other large cities, ethnic groups tend to cluster in certain areas, such as Chinatown, Little Italy, and Harlem. All tend to keep their gene pools closed, even though they are part of a larger population. The result of all such cultural segregation is to limit the openness of a population's gene pool by creating several subpopulation gene pools, which are then kept "protected."

Despite such restrictions on a population's gene pool, whether imposed by the environment or by social values, modern societies tend to favor open gene pools much more than did societies of a century or even a few decades ago. That is especially true in the world's major cities, where large populations of mixed racial and cultural types abound. Here the gene pools are potentially more open to the rapid inflow of new genes which add variations to the population.

Because variation results from intermarriage, racial distinctions within genetically busy populations sometimes become blurred. For instance, the Hawaiians, once a genetically and culturally distinct group, have all but lost their original identity. There is but a handful of genetically "pure" Hawaiians left. Their homeland is a vast melting pot of Chinese, Japanese, Hawaiian, and other cultures. The same is happening in many parts of the world because of new social values, rapid communication of ideas, and the ease of crossing distances of several thousand miles in only a few hours. Is such blurring of cultural and racial distinctions good or bad? Who are you or I to say?

TRENDS IN CULTURAL EVOLUTION
Even though there are big differences between living in a limestone cave and in the White House, human beings have changed hardly at all in appearance over the past 25,000 years. Our limbs and teeth are the same now as then, although we have enriched our lives vastly and increased our life spans through nutrition and shelter.

The major difference between people living today and those living 100,000 years ago is not language, behavior, or culture, but something more deeply rooted. Populations of our distant ancestors were biologically adapted to their environment. If the environment changed for the worse, a population either stuck it out and evolved suitable adaptations or it packed up and moved on to a more favorable environment.

Today, if we don't like the environment, we use our engineering technology to change it or our medical technology to alter our ability to cope. When astronauts walk on the Moon or orbit Earth in a space station, they carry their Earth environment of oxygen, air pressure, and gas exchange systems with them in an airtight cocoon. We now have the technology to pack up our environment and establish a colony in space or on Mars, for instance, within a closed ecological system.

Art is an aspect of cultural evolution. The paintings so beautifully done on rock walls of limestone caves in France and Spain 30,000 years ago, and on rock walls of Brazil's Pedra Furada rock shelter 33,000 years ago, were not done for resale but were painted for a deadly serious purpose—to assure success in the hunt. Yet those early artists surely took pride in their work and looked on it with a sense of beauty as well as function. Since then we have raised that sense of appreciation to the point where art is beauty for the sake of beauty alone.

When we speak of cultural evolution, we mean the handing down of knowledge and information from one generation to the next. This transmission of knowledge is very valuable to our species, but each generation has the choice of carrying on earlier traditions or abandoning them. We do not attend the opera, ride a bicycle, or watch a tennis match on television because our genes tell us to. We do these things because we are taught to do them, and such behaviors are part of our cultural tradition. The transmission of culture from one generation to the next is an intellectual affair, not a genetic one, and culture is free to evolve as rapidly or as slowly as we choose to change it. The result may be an explosive growth of knowledge in an amazingly short time, compared with the rate at which biological evolution creeps along.

Like biological evolution, cultural evolution also brings about change between a population and its environment. For example, today environmentalists form a worldwide group united in their concern over preserving the quality of the environment. Often they are in conflict with paper companies that pollute the air for hundreds of miles around a factory, nuclear power plants that produce high-level radioactive wastes that will be around for tens of thousands of years, and chemical plants that dump their wastes into rivers and the oceans. The environmentalists' concern is that increasing abuse of the environment is harming the quality of human life and the future of the planet, whereas the chief concern of big business is quick financial profit, often with little or no concern for whether the environment is damaged. Which side you happen to be on affects the way you behave in relation to the environment. There are those who pollute and litter, and those who clean up and pick up. Such concerns, or lack of them, are part of the cultural baggage that we carry with us and pass on to our children through example and education.

Today virtually all of the world's people belong to societies that are regulated by cultural values, philosophical attitudes, religious beliefs, and laws. Small populations usually are more easily regulated because their members tend to control one another's behavior and are not tolerant of social misfits. Big populations such as those making up a huge city are not so easily regulated. The large numbers of people and many variations in their outlooks on life and in their social behavior make the regulation of behavior more difficult. At the same time it becomes easier for social misfits, who are unwilling or unable to control their behavior according to the rules agreed on by most members of society, to become lost in the crowd.

What answers can we come up with when we ask what directions cultural evolution of the world's populations is taking now and will take in the future? And what will be the resulting effect on the *quality* of human life? We must consider the present trend of large populations rapidly growing still larger, as is happening in many parts of the world, especially in Third World countries.

HUMAN POPULATION GROWTH

The world's human population is growing at a rate that many scholars find alarming. At the time the Paleo-Indians crossed over into the Americas from Asia, the total world population probably was only about 5 million, the present population of Philadelphia. By the time of Julius

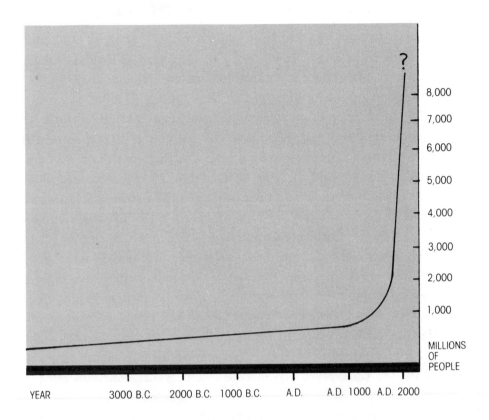

8,000
7,000
6,000
5,000
4,000
3,000
2,000
1,000

MILLIONS
OF
PEOPLE

YEAR   3000 B.C.   2000 B.C. 1000 B.C.   A.D.   A.D. 1000 A.D. 2000

The human population growth curve is on a steep rise that alarms many people. No known population of organisms has ever grown at such a rate without experiencing a major change. Compare the rate of population growth from 3000 B.C. to A.D. 1500, then from 1500 to 2000.

Caesar, the world population had reached about 250 million and continued to grow, reaching 500 million by the year 1650. But widespread famine and disease often slowed population growth. The leading killer diseases were tuberculosis, typhus, plague, and smallpox. During the Middle Ages smallpox killed one out of every four people. In one year, 1720, plague killed forty thousand people living in the French city of Marseilles.

Today in some countries, modern medicine and standards of hygiene have lowered the death rate, while birth rates continue to climb. In the

United States our rate of new births plus the inflow of legal and illegal immigrants is keeping our national population growing. Each year we add the population equivalent of four Washington, D.C.'s.

By 1970 the world population had passed the 3.6 billion mark and by mid-1988 it had passed 5 billion. By the year 2020 it is estimated to pass 8 billion. The more people there are, the faster the world population grows. Around the year 1850 it took 150 years for the world population to double. Today the doubling time is about 40 years, and in about 3 decades it may be only 15 years. What all these numbers mean is that the world population is growing at a rate that is out of control. The question is not *should* we stop it, but *how* do we stop it? More and more people mean increases in the production of food, houses, energy; billions of tons of manufactured goods, and much more pollution. As our numbers continue to increase, what will happen to the quality of life?

Such questions must concern us even if we do not yet have the answers. On Chesapeake Bay overdevelopment has contaminated the water quality and degraded shoreline ecology. In the Florida Everglades human competition for water and habitat has evicted or destroyed the local populations of many wildlife species, including the endangered Florida panther and peregrine falcon. On a worldwide basis, if population demands on the environment continue—and they are sure to—increased cutting of the planet's tropical forests could cause 25 percent of all wildlife species to disappear within the next 50 years.

Even though we lack many of the answers about the effects of a runaway world population, we have a long cultural tradition and the intelligence to guide both our cultural and biological evolution into the future. Our technology in communication enables us to send whatever messages we may consider important or desirable to all parts of the world at the speed of light. In so doing, we demonstrate our ability to guide our collective cultural evolution. In recent years our medical technology has given us the power to change the human population's gene pool through genetic engineering. It is now possible to remove unwanted genes from an individual's genetic package or to add a needed gene that may be lacking. It also is possible to treat people with genetic disease so that they may lead a normal life. But some people are opposed to such "tampering" with life.

Without treatment, natural selection tends to remove many genetically damaged individuals from the population and so prevents their defective gene(s) from entering the gene pool. By keeping such people alive with medical technology, we are keeping their defective, and unwanted, genes in the population's gene pool, with the result that the genes can be passed on to those yet to be born. Is not that action also "tampering" with life? We come to the aid of such genetically diseased people for "humanitarian" reasons, we tell ourselves, through consideration for the individual. But what of consideration for society? Can we overlook that concern? Nature does not perform humanitarian acts.

We are now wrestling with a cultural monster of our own making—technology. Are we to control it, or is it to control us? Whichever path we take, we will be directing our future rather than passively letting the accidents of nature decide everything for us. Among the countless other species with which we share this planet, we alone have the intelligence to plan our future, and indirectly theirs, as well. Whether we have the wisdom to plan it well remains to be seen—not by us but by people many generations farther along the evolutionary line.

What about the far-distant future of *Homo sapiens*? Will human beings live forever? The idea that we have raised ourselves above the influence of evolution by natural forces is as foolish as belief in the Tooth Fairy. Within a million years or so, according to Margulis, we can expect to have become extinct as a species, having given rise to one or more descendant species. That can be reasonably expected based on what we know about all other species since the beginning of life on planet Earth, and it is a fascinating thought.

Are we alone in the Universe? This question looms larger than ever today. If we can sample the alien dust of another world, what hidden secrets may we not discover? If we scan the radio waves from a distant galaxy, what may we not hear if we listen closely? If we probe into the chemistry of life's origin, what may we not discern about its possibility elsewhere in the Universe? The search for life beyond the Earth is the driving force of the new science of exobiology.

—Cyril Ponnamperuma, 1972

13
Life and Evolution on Other Planets

OF WORLDS BEYOND OUR OWN

How many life-supporting planets exist out there in the dark? To begin, let's consider just one small thimbleful of space, our home galaxy the Milky Way with its 500 billion or so stars. One of those stars is called Barnard's Star. It is a red dwarf nearly 6 light-years away, or 36 trillion miles. For 40 years the American astronomer Peter van de Kamp studied that faint star and eventually found that it traced a wobbly path in its journey through space. He reasoned that there must be a planet revolving around the star and that the wobble occurred because both star and planet circled a point called the center of mass. Earth and the Moon revolve about a common center of mass located just inside Earth's crust. If we were able to track Earth's path from afar, we would find that it, too, traces a wobbly path.

Since van de Kamp's discovery, several other wobbly stars have been detected, and it is suggested that they also have planetary companions. But how many of them have conditions suitable for life of some sort?

For a planet to support life, any kind of life, it must meet certain conditions. Distance from its local star is one. If a planet is too near its local star (like Mercury, for instance), the planet will receive so much energy that complex life-producing molecules—amino acid and protein molecules, for instance—either could not form or, if they did form, could not remain stable. At the other extreme, if a planet is too far away from its local star (like Pluto, for instance), the planet will be too cold for life, receiving too little energy for chemical reactions to proceed rapidly enough to build complex groups of life-giving molecules.

There are other considerations for a habitable planet. Mass, for example. Mass plays an important role in several ways, including the determination of surface gravity. The hefty dinosaurs never would have made it on a planet with a surface gravity twice as strong as Earth's. They would have collapsed under their own weight, unable to move about. Mass also determines whether a planet is able to hold on to an atmosphere, and the kinds of elements present in that atmosphere. Stephen H. Dole estimates that a suitable mass range for a habitable planet may lie between 0.4 and 2.35 times Earth's mass. That would mean a planetary diameter of between 6,200 miles (compared with Earth's diameter of 7,900 miles) and 16,000 miles, assuming a rock makeup similar to Earth's.

A planet's rate of rotation and the amount its polar axis is tilted toward or away from its local star are important temperature regulators that determine the degree of habitability of certain zones on the planet.

The kind of star the planet has as its local Sun also is important to the evolution of life on the planet. The star could be a fiercely burning blue giant star with a life span of only a few million years; it could be a Sunlike star with a life span of about 10 billion years; it could be a feebly burning red dwarf star with a very much longer life span; or it could be any number of erratic stars whose energy outputs vary greatly.

The only technological civilization we know of is our own. Using ourselves as a model, we may assume that it takes some 3 billion years for a technological civilization to evolve. What this means is that if we set out to search for intelligent life elsewhere in the universe, we should rule out not only erratic stars but all stars with short life spans, those measured in only a few million years. We will make better use of our time by searching among Sunlike stars and the red dwarfs, both of which have relatively long life spans.

For complex life to evolve there must be enough time and the right conditions: for an atmosphere to form; for simple organic molecules to form and build into proteinlike substances; and for prebiological cells to form, cells capable of evolving into biological cells, after which evolution may take off in a grand style—at least it did at the turn of the Cambrian Period on Earth.

Many astronomers suspect that there are billions of other planets in the Milky Way that have the right conditions for complex life to have evolved. They further suspect that many of them could support settlements suitable for human beings, settlements in which we might feel quite at home. It they are right, then the billions of other galaxies beyond our own probably have countless planets that support life and where the wheels of evolution are now turning.

According to astronomers Carl Sagan and Frank Drake, "If the origin of life is highly probable, if there are billions of years of evolution available on each [habitable] planet, and if even a small fraction of technical civilizations pass safely through technological adolescence, the number of technological civilizations in the Galaxy today might be very large. . . . Our best guess is that there are a million civilizations in our galaxy at or beyond Earth's present level of technological development."

If evolution has had the long time necessary to fashion complex life forms on any of those other planets in our galaxy or beyond, the courses that it followed would not be the same courses that evolution has followed on Earth. That is not because the laws of physics and chemistry are different out there but because the infinite chance occurrences that make up evolution are too vast in number to be exactly repeated on any two planets. But there are bound to be similarities.

A meteorite that fell in Australia in 1969 contained molecules of methanol and amino acids, evidence that Earthlike chemical evolution takes place elsewhere in the universe. In addition, radio astronomers have identified about fifty chemical compounds in space, old-fashioned Earth compounds, such as carbon monoxide, ammonia, water vapor, and formaldehyde, among others.

This suggests that we might expect to find certain general biochemical similarities on other habitable planets. For example, since hydrogen is by far the most abundant element in the universe, we can expect hydrogen to be an important part of living matter wherever life has evolved. To the best of our knowledge, water is the only major source of hydrogen, so we can expect living organisms throughout space to have some means of breaking down water molecules. In the process they would use the hydrogen and liberate oxygen.

We also could expect to find certain general similarities among the organic molecules built up early in a planet's life history, since water, ammonia, and methane appear to be among the most plentiful atmospheric compounds produced during the early stages of Earthlike planets. But what happens to those molecules as they evolve chemically and then biologically over the next billions of years is much harder to say.

We can be certain that salmon, squirrels, parrots, and people will not be found on any other planet in the universe. But we can be just as certain that there is a nearly infinite variety of life forms out there that swim, crawl, walk on two or more legs, and fly through an atmosphere. After all, eyes evolved many times on Earth in groups as different as worms, squids, insects, and elephants. So did wings, in insects, reptiles, birds, and bats. All are groups with very different ancestry. The tendency of such different groups to evolve similar structures to do one job is called convergent evolution. If it happened here, there is every reason to suppose that it can happen anywhere.

We can also expect intelligence to evolve in some of those advanced organisms, intelligence that could build a complex cultural tradition, including science and engineering. Since we did not invent scientific laws and the engineering principles based on those laws, but only discovered and exploited them, can we reasonably expect the engineering marvels on other Earthlike planets to be basically similar to those of our own design?

Again, while we may eventually find and communicate with intelligent life elsewhere in the Galaxy, we can expect to find certain similarities but not duplicates of even a single species that has evolved on Earth.

Loren Eiseley, in his book *The Immense Journey,* echoes that thought eloquently in these words:

> Life, even cellular life, may exist out yonder in the dark. But high or low in nature, it will not wear the shape of man. That shape is the evolutionary product of a strange, long wandering through the attics of the forest roof, and so great are the chances of failure, that nothing precisely and identically human is likely ever to come that way again.
>
> Lights come and go in the night sky. Men, troubled at last by the things they build, may toss in their sleep and dream bad dreams, or lie awake while the meteors whisper greenly overhead. But nowhere in all space or on a thousand worlds will there be men to share our loneliness. There may be wisdom; there may be power; somewhere across space great instruments, handled by strange manipulative organs, may stare vainly at our floating cloud wrack, their owners yearning as we yearn. Nevertheless, in the nature of life and in the principles of evolution we have had our answer. Of men elsewhere, and beyond, there will be none forever.

OUR FUTURE IN SPACE

Once begun more than 3 billion years ago, life took hold on this planet and has never let go. Species evolve and die, but life persists. As we saw in earlier chapters, each time there has been an environmental catastrophe—the oxygen revolution of the Precambrian, or the mass extinctions at the end of the Permian and Cretaceous periods—evolution has rebounded with renewed vigor and invention. The great dying among the amphibians opened the environment to reptiles, then the death of the dinosaurs cleared the way for the rise of the primates.

Some have wondered if an all-out nuclear war would finish off life on Earth. It would lay ruin to many of its forms but would hardly dent life itself. Life is here to stay—at least for a cosmic while—and will keep on evolving on this planet until the ultimate Earth-shaking drama occurs.

That drama is due in about 5 billion years when the Sun will have used up its hydrogen fuel and, according to the laws of physics, will turn into a red giant star. At that stage in its evolution, the Sun will swell up and engulf Mercury and Venus. Not even the hardiest and most protected microbes on Earth will be able to withstand the awful heat as the oceans boil away and the rock crust melts. After that the Sun is destined to again collapse, but this time with no new outpourings of energy to warm Earth and the remaining planets. Eventually the Sun will evolve into a cold black dwarf continuing to wheel through space, carrying with it seven dark cold worlds, Earth among them, lifeless and barren of any trace of a proud past.

By then *Homo sapiens* will have become extinct, possibly after having coasted through millions of years of arrested evolution as a living fossil like the horseshoe crab, or after having given rise to one or more new species. But before the very end, the master molecules of DNA of certain surviving species will be molecular missiles awaiting some chance, or planned, event that could dispatch them across the depths of space to other hospitable worlds.

THE COLONIZATION OF SPACE

Although planet Earth a few billion years from now will not reveal the past history of the life it once harbored, other worlds beyond the dead Sun almost certainly will perform that role, for the forces of evolution are one day bound to push Earth life out among the stars.

We have taken our first baby steps into space by sending astronauts to the Moon, and others will be sent to Mars. Science fiction writers have spun thousands of tales of men and women voyaging among the stars in massive spaceships, visiting and colonizing strange planets with exotic life forms.

Since we are prisoners of our environmental requirements and of biological time, it would require hundreds of generations of space travel for colonists to explore even the local suburbs of our galaxy. Furthermore, the tens of thousands of colonists would need enormous spacecrafts which would have to be closed ecological systems housing millions of tons of cultural and biological baggage in the form of libraries, scientific laboratories, hospitals, vast gardens, and numerous species of plants and animals. In short, we would need to carve out representative samples of our environment and move them through the cosmos as home for as many generations as it took to find other planets with environments suitable for human life. Considering the staggering expense of such a project, it seems unlikely that a single nation could afford to pay the cost, or that a group of nations could ever agree on how the job should be done.

But suppose for a moment that the bill could be paid. How long would it take to colonize our local galaxy? Edward R. Harrison, of the University of Massachusetts, paints the following scenario. A single massive spaceship sets out on a journey across 10 light-years of space to a habitable planet. Traveling at one-thousandth the speed of light, the voyage would last 10,000 years. The colonists occupy the planet and remain there for another 10,000 years before their descendants set out on a second voyage. Over the tens and hundreds of thousands of years of wave after wave of voyages, life would spread among the planets at a rate of 10 light-years every 30,000 years. The entire galaxy would be colonized in only 50 million years. Recall that the dinosaurs were around three times that long. Throughout that time the many descendants of the original colonists would have evolved into new species, with *Homo sapiens* becoming extinct, or possibly hanging on in a state of arrested evolution on one or more planets.

If *Homo sapiens* doesn't colonize other parts of the Galaxy before the Sun dies, then what representatives of our planet will carry our message out among the stars? Long after we are gone as a species, other species with intelligence and technologies far superior to ours are bound to have evolved on Earth and carried on in a grand new style of their own where *Homo sapiens* left off. Such relay evolution has been the pattern in the past.

In some way unknown to us, and probably even unimaginable, organisms high or low in the evolutionary scheme of things are likely to expand beyond the confines of Earth's biosphere. By that time the numerous species then alive, and endless more to come, will count their numbered days until the Sun dies and snuffs out all living matter on Earth. But life itself will have survived and begun the exploration of evolutionary opportunities in the remotest parts of the Galaxy.

Glossary

ACCRETION   A clumping process of matter that may have caused the planets and their moons to have formed out of the original matter that led to the formation of the Solar System. That matter probably consisted of ice, rock, and metals, the particles being drawn together, or accreted, by gravity.

ADAPTATION   The condition of a plant or animal population being in tune with its environment, or its ability to adjust to changes in the environment (scarcity of food or change in climate, for example). Sometimes the environmental changes are so severe that no individuals of the population can survive, and the population dies out. In other cases, when the change is less severe, certain individuals that are "fitter" than the others are able to survive and pass on their fitness to their offspring. In that way, the population as a group becomes adapted to the new environment.

ADAPTIVE RADIATION   The spreading of populations into different environments with the result that each population evolves unique adaptations that may give rise to new species. The adaptive radiation of reptiles and primates are examples of such speeded-up speciation.

AMINO ACIDS   Complex molecules that were among the first molecules of life some 4 billion or so years ago when Earth had developed a solid crust. Amino acids contain carbon, oxygen, nitrogen, and hydrogen. These molecules are the building blocks of proteins. There are about 20 different kinds of amino acids.

AMPHIBIANS   That animal group that spends part of its life cycle in water and part on land, including frogs and salamanders, for example. Amphibians lay their eggs in water, where the eggs hatch; the young are fishlike and breathe through gills. Later the young develop into land-dwellers with lungs and four legs.

ANIMAL   Any multicellular organism made up of eukaryotic cells lacking cell walls, which usually moves about, and which usually takes in food through a mouth cavity. The animal kingdom includes not only mammals, reptiles, amphibians, and birds, but sponges, jellyfish, corals, worms, clams, insects, and starfish.

ANTHROPOLOGY   The "study of man," including social organization, customs and beliefs, language, and physical aspects of people living today and who lived long ago.

ARCHAEOLOGY   The study of the history and cultures of peoples who lived in the past by discovering and interpreting the material remains they left behind.

ARRESTED EVOLUTION   A relatively slow rate of evolution of a given species within a larger group such as mammals or clams, for example. Arrested evolution seems to occur in those species that are not highly specialized; for instance, species that can tolerate a wide temperature range and have a wide-ranging diet.

ARTHROPODS   The animal group that includes 80 percent of all known animal species. Almost all arthropods have hard outside skeletons (like grasshoppers, lobsters, and spiders), have jointed legs that enable them to crawl, burrow, or swim, and have bodies divided into segments.

ARTIFACT   Any object, including tools and weapons, made by human beings. Artifacts include such items as stone tools, projectile points, harpoons, and arrowheads, for example.

ASTEROIDS   Any of millions of rock-metal fragments ranging in size from a fraction of a foot to several scores of yards or more across and traveling around the Sun in orbits between Mars and Jupiter. Collisions between asteroids may cause some of the broken pieces to be flung far and wide, some reaching Earth where they burn up in the atmosphere as meteors or strike the surface as meteorites.

ASTRONOMY   The science dealing with celestial bodies, their distances, luminosities, sizes, motions, relative positions, composition, and structure. The word comes from the Greek and means the "arrangement of the stars."

ATOM   The smallest possible piece of an element that can take part in a chemical reaction. An atom retains all the properties of its element.

BINARY FISSION   The process of a single-celled organism—an amoeba or bacterium, for example—dividing in two and producing a new individual identical to the parent individual with the same DNA and RNA. Also called simple division.

BIOGENESIS   The principle that life arises only from living things.

BLACK DWARF   A star that has passed through the white dwarf stage and is radiating so little energy that it can no longer be observed directly.

BLUE GIANT   An especially massive, large, and luminous star, such as Rigel (in Orion), which is seen to shine with a bluish white light. The core temperatures and surface temperatures of these short-lived stars are many times higher than those of less massive stars such as the Sun.

BOTANIST   Any scientist who specializes in the study of plants.

CAMBRIAN PERIOD That geological time period in the Paleozoic Era spanning 80 million years and that lasted from about 580 million to 500 million years ago.

CARBONIFEROUS PERIOD That geologic time period in the Paleozoic Era spanning 55 million years and that lasted from about 345 million years ago to 290 million years ago.

CELL The smallest organized unit of living matter recognized by biologists. All living organisms are composed of cells. Some organisms, such as a paramecium, are a single cell.

CENOZOIC ERA That geologic time period that began about 65 million years ago and that continues to the present. It is divided into two periods—the Tertiary and Quaternary. It also is called the Age of Mammals.

CLIMATE A region's weather averaged over a long span of time. From the Greek word *klima,* meaning "slope" or "incline," and referring to the degree of slant of the Sun's rays relative to Earth's surface.

COLD-BLOODED Having a body temperature that changes with the temperature of the environment. Reptiles are cold-blooded animals. Warm-blooded animals, such as mammals, maintain a constant body temperature and so enjoy a survival advantage over cold-blooded species.

CRETACEOUS PERIOD That geologic time period in the Mesozoic Era spanning some 72 million years and that lasted from 138 million years ago to about 66 million years ago.

CRO-MAGNON Early *Homo sapiens* who were more modern than and replaced the Neanderthals about 30,000 years ago. The earliest Cro-Magnon groups probably came from South Africa about 100,000 years ago. Cro-Magnon populations were in North America at least 12,000 years ago, possibly much earlier, having crossed over a land bridge that linked Siberia to Alaska.

CRUST The thin layer of rock covering the surface of our planet, reaching about 6 miles (9 kilometers) deep beneath the oceans to about 37 miles (60 kilometers) deep beneath the continents. Most of the continents are made up of a granite-type rock.

CULTURE The customs, equipment, techniques, manufactures, ideas, language, and beliefs of a people.

DENSITY Mass per unit volume, or the amount of matter contained in a given volume of space, and expressed as grams per cubic centimeter. Water, for example, has a density of 1 gram per cubic centimeter.

DEVONIAN PERIOD That geologic time period in the Paleozoic Era spanning some 55 million years and that lasted from about 400 million years ago to 345 million years ago. This period is known as the Age of Fishes.

DINOSAUR Any of the many extinct reptiles that lived during the Mesozoic era, some of which reached gigantic size. For reasons still unknown, all of the dinosaurs had become extinct by about 65 million years ago, at the end of the Cretaceous Period.

DIVERSITY The many different kinds of animal and plant species that have evolved over the past 3 billion or so years. Scientists have classified more than 1.2 million different animal species and at least 500,000 species of plants. Each year thousands of newly discovered species are added to the lists.

DNA (deoxyribonucleic acid) The substance of genes and the carrier of genetic information in cells, and a supervisor of the manufacture of protein.

ELECTRON A negative unit of electricity that is part of all atoms. Clouds of electrons surround the nuclei of atoms. The mass of an electron is only a small fraction of the mass of a proton (1/1,840 that of the hydrogen atom).

ELEMENT   A substance made up entirely of the same kinds of atoms. Such a substance cannot be broken down into a simpler substance by chemical means. Examples are gold, oxygen, lead, and chlorine.

ENERGY   That property of an object enabling it to do work. Stars emit huge amounts of energy in the forms of light, heat, radio waves, X rays, and ultraviolet rays, for example.

EOCENE EPOCH   That geologic time block in the Tertiary Period that lasted about 16 million years, beginning 54 million years ago and ending 38 million years ago.

EROSION   The long-term effects of heat, water, wind, ice, and acid rain that may chip away or chemically dissolve solid rock. The chipped away particles are called sediments. Sediments may be formed by mechanical action or by chemical or biochemical processes.

EUKARYOTES   Cells with an organized nucleus enclosed within a membrane.

EVOLUTION   The various patterns of biological change that ultimately cause the success (adaptation) or failure (extinction) of species and produce new species of plants and animals. As it has in the past, biological evolution continues to take place today. Charles Darwin and Alfred Russell Wallace are credited with developing the basic principles of evolution.

EXTINCTION   The total disappearance of an entire species or higher group of plants or animals. Once a species has become extinct, it is gone forever.

FAULT   A crack or break in Earth's crustal rock. Two surfaces along a fault may strain against each other until the pressure is so great that the two surfaces slip, or snap. The snapping action causes an earthquake. The San Andreas Fault in California is the dividing line between two great blocks of Earth's crust that press against each other and cause earthquakes.

FOSSILS The remains of once-living plants or animals. Fossils may be bits of bone or teeth or even footprints or other imprints left from long ago. Most fossils are found in sedimentary rock and usually are more than 10,000 years old.

GALAXY A vast collection of stars, gas, and dust held together gravitationally. Spiral galaxies, the brightest of all galaxies, have a dense nucleus with less dense spiral arms. Our galaxy, the Milky Way, is a spiral galaxy containing some 500 billion stars.

GENE That biological unit of inheritance that determines a particular trait, such as hair color, tallness, and general physical appearance of an individual.

GENUS A broad grouping of organisms, all of which have certain characteristics in common but which belong to different species. For example, there are various species of the genus *Homo.* Modern humans belong to the species *Homo sapiens,* which means "wise man," while *Homo habilis* refers to a humanlike species that lived long ago. According to the principles of evolution, all members of the same genus are descended from a fairly recent common ancestor.

GEOLOGIC TIME The time that has passed since Earth's history began. It involves millions and billions of years, very much longer than our imagination can grasp. Geologic eras include relatively larger blocks of time than do geologic periods, and geologic epochs are the shortest intervals of all.

GLACIER Any mass of moving land ice formed out of compacted snow. There are eight principal forms of glaciers.

GLUCOSE A sugar-food used by plants and animals alike. Glucose is produced by green plants when they combine carbon dioxide and water vapor in the presence of light as an energy source. In the process, the green plant gives off oxygen as a by-product to the air.

GRAVITATION The force of attraction between any two or more objects in the universe, no matter how large or small. The attraction between any two objects in the universe is directly proportional to their mass and inversely proportional to the square of the distance between them. The greater the mass, the greater the force of attraction; the greater the distance, the less the force of attraction.

GRAVITY   The gravitational force between Earth, for instance, and any object on its surface or within its gravitational field.

HABITAT   The environment in which a species lives, together with all the plant and animal organisms to be found there.

HOMINID   Any primate in the human family. Modern humans are the only surviving hominids. A group known as *Australopithecus* may have been the first true hominids; they lived as long ago as 5.5 million years, in the late Tertiary Period.

HOMINOID   That primate branch that includes humans and apes.

HOMO ERECTUS   A group of hominids that were clearly human, but not yet modern humans. *Homo erectus* hunted, lived in caves, and knew the art of starting fire. The name means "upright man."

HOMO HABILIS   A humanlike species that lived in Africa and Asia some 1.8 million years ago and that gave rise to *Homo erectus*. *Homo habilis* means "able man."

HOMO SAPIENS   The group name of modern humans. It means "wise man."

ICE AGE   Any extended period of time during which a substantial portion of Earth's surface is covered by "permanent" ice. There have been seven known major ice ages during the past 700,000 years, with the last ice age reaching its peak about 18,000 years ago.

IGNEOUS ROCK   Rock formed when molten material flows up from deeper parts of Earth's crust and solidifies either within the crust or at the surface. Of the three kinds of rock described in this book, igneous rock makes up about 65 percent of Earth's crust. Igneous rock may be either intrusive (hidden below Earth's surface) or extrusive (exposed at the surface).

INVERTEBRATES   Any animal species lacking a backbone. The first animals to evolve were invertebrates. Early invertebrates that lived in the ancient seas included sponges, trilobites, brachiopods, and graptolites.

JURASSIC PERIOD   That geologic time period in the Mesozoic Era spanning about 57 million years and that lasted from about 195 million years ago to 138 million years ago. This period is called the Age of Reptiles.

LAVA   Molten rock that is forced out of a volcano or out of cracks in Earth's crust and hardens at the surface.

LIGHT-YEAR (L.Y.)   The distance that light travels in one year, at the rate of 299,000 kilometers (186,000) miles per second, which is about 10 trillion kilometers (6 trillion miles).

MAGMA   Fluid rock material originating in the deeper parts of Earth's crust. It is capable of forcing its way up through solid rock and, when flowing out over the surface, it is then called lava. Lava solidifies into igneous rock.

MAMMAL   Any vertebrate animal that has warm blood and a covering of hair, that gives birth to its young (with two exceptions), and that suckles its young.

MASS   A given quantity of matter of any kind, or the total quantity of matter contained in an object.

MEMBRANE   A protective and porous "jacket" enclosing cells. A membrane separates an organism's inside environment from the outside environment. Tiny holes in the membrane let certain "food" molecules enter the cell to be used as building blocks for growth and as a source of energy. The holes also let waste matter escape to the outside. The development of a membrane was an important step in the evolution of the first biological cells some 3 billion years or so ago.

MESOZOIC ERA   The time of "middle life," spanning some 160 million years and usually broken down into three periods—the Triassic, Jurassic, and Cretaceous. The dinosaurs reached their peak during the late Mesozoic.

METAMORPHIC ROCK   Any rock mass of Earth's crust that has been recognizably changed in texture and/or mineral composition by heat or chemically active fluids. Metamorphic rock makes up about 27 percent of Earth's rocks.

METEORITES   Pieces of rock or rock-metal from interplanetary space that have survived their journey down through Earth's atmosphere without burning up. While still in space such objects are called "meteoroids," and the brief flaming light streak they make as they heat up in the atmosphere is called a "meteor."

MIOCENE EPOCH   That geologic time block in the Tertiary Period lasting some 19 million years, beginning about 26 million years ago and ending 7 million years ago.

MITOCHONDRION   Structures within a cell that are associated with energy production.

MOLECULE   Two or more atoms joined to form a compound, such as two hydrogen atoms joined to one oxygen atom to form one molecule of water (H_2O).

MUTATION   A random, or chance, change in a plant or animal's genes that makes the organism different in one or more ways from its parents. Most mutations are harmful, although many throughout the course of evolution have proven to be beneficial. Mutations may be passed on to offspring.

NATURAL SELECTION   The act of the environment favoring for survival those individuals who are the fittest, or best adapted to environmental conditions. While less fit individuals tend to be selected against and do not survive, those who are more fit live to reproduce offspring and so pass their fitness on to the next generation.

NEANDERTHAL MAN   Large-jawed people who lived across Europe into the Near East and into central Asia. About five feet tall, they were strong and had large bones. They became extinct about 35,000 years ago.

NUCLEAR FUSION   The union of atomic nuclei and, as a result, the building of the nuclei of more massive atoms. Hydrogen nuclei in the core of the Sun fuse and build up the nuclei of helium atoms. In the process large amounts of energy are emitted, thus accounting for the Sun's energy output.

OLIGOCENE EPOCH   That geologic time block in the Tertiary Period that lasted about 12 million years, beginning some 38 million years ago and ending 26 million years ago.

ORBIT   The path one celestial object traces as it moves around another to which it is attracted by the force of gravitation. Earth and the other planets of the Solar System all have their own orbits around the Sun. The Moon travels in an orbit around Earth, and the Sun travels in an orbit around the nucleus of our galaxy.

ORDOVICIAN PERIOD   That geologic time period in the Paleozoic Era spanning 60 million years and that lasted from about 500 million years ago to about 440 million years ago.

PALEOCENE EPOCH   That geologic time block in the Tertiary Period that lasted about 12 million years, beginning some 66 million years ago and ending 54 million years ago.

PALEO-INDIANS   Any of those groups of people who entered the Americas from Asia up to 5,000 B.C. and who hunted now extinct animals. Most researchers think that the Paleo-Indians crossed over to the New World over a sprawling land bridge that existed near the end of the last glacial period. Recent evidence suggests that Paleo-Indians may have been in South America at least 30,000 years ago, and possibly much earlier.

PALEONTOLOGIST   A scientist who specializes in the recovery and study of fossils.

PALEOZOIC ERA   The period of ancient life, predating the Mesozoic Era and spanning 325 million years of Earth's history. The Paleozoic is made up of six geologic periods.

PANGAEA   The single supercontinent that existed about 220 million years ago when all the land masses were merged into one. By about 135 million years ago, Pangaea had broken up into a northern half, called Laurasia, and a southern half, called Gondwana, which had drifted apart.

PEAT   A material formed in swamps from dead trees and other vegetation that has been packed in layers over many years. Peat bogs are common in many parts of the world today, and dried peat is sometimes used as fuel. Peat represents the first stage in the formation of coal.

PERMIAN PERIOD   That geologic time period in the Paleozoic Era spanning about 45 million years and that lasted from about 290 million years ago to 245 million years ago.

PHOTOSYNTHESIS   The ability of green plants to build up molecules of sugar out of water vapor and carbon dioxide of the atmosphere in the presence of sunlight and the green pigment chlorophyll. In the process oxygen is given off as a by-product. Green plants supply all of the world's living organisms with food.

PLANETARY SYSTEM   Any star accompanied by one or more planets. The Solar System is presumably only one of many planetary systems in our and other galaxies.

PLANETESIMALS   Clumps of solid matter that formed out of the solar disk material in the early years of the Solar System. The planetesimals were made up of rock or rock mixed with iron and other metals. Billions of these planetesimals plunged into Earth and the other planets and their moons during the first 700 million years, producing great heat and, later, many craters.

PLANETS Celestial objects that shine by reflected light from a star around which they are held gravitationally captive and revolve. There are nine known primary planets in the Solar System.

PLASTID A class of cell parts found in green plants. Chloroplasts are bundles of green pigment associated with photosynthesis.

PLEISTOCENE EPOCH That geologic time block in the Tertiary Period that lasted nearly 2 million years, beginning 2 million years ago and ending 0.1 million years ago.

PLIOCENE EPOCH That geologic time block in the Tertiary Period that lasted 5 million years, beginning 7 million years ago and ending 2 million years ago.

PRECAMBRIAN ERA That geologic time span from 4.6 billion years ago—the estimated age of Earth—to 580 million years ago. The Precambrian is generally viewed as the time when life was firmly establishing itself on Earth.

PRESSURE A measurement of force per unit area.

PRIMATE That branch of mammals that includes tree shrews, lemurs and tarsiers, New World monkeys, Old World monkeys, gibbons, orangutans, gorillas, chimpanzees, and modern humans and their apelike ancestors.

PROKARYOTES A single cell lacking a nucleus enclosed within a membrane. Bacteria are prokaryotes.

PROTEIN A class of large molecules made up of amino acids and that serve as an energy source in all living things and as structural materials.

PROTON A fundamental particle present in the nucleus of all atoms. A proton has a positive charge of electricity equal in strength to the negative charge of an electron, but a proton is 1,840 times more massive than an electron.

PROTOSTAR   A newly forming star that has not yet begun to radiate visible energy as a result of fusing hydrogen nuclei into helium nuclei in the star's core region.

QUATERNARY PERIOD   That geologic time period in the Cenezoic Era that began 2 million years ago and includes the present.

RACE   Can be thought of as a group of populations within any species that have certain physical and genetic characteristics in common, which set that group of populations apart from all other populations of the same species.

RADIOACTIVE DATING   The natural decay, at known rates, of certain radioactive elements such as uranium, potassium, and carbon into other elements. For instance, half the amount of uranium-238 in a sample decays into lead-206 in 4,510 million years; half the amount of carbon-14 in a sample decays into nitrogen-14 in 5,600 years.

RECENT EPOCH   That geologic time block in the Quarternary Period that began 100,000 years ago and that we live in now.

RED DWARF   A star with relatively little mass and a low surface temperature (about 3,000 kelvins), which causes the star to shine with a reddish light.

RED GIANT   An enormous star that shines with a reddish light because of its relatively low surface temperature (about 3,000 kelvins). It is now thought that most stars go through a red-giant stage after they exhaust their core hydrogen and the core collapses gravitationally. The star then swells up and becomes a red giant.

REPTILE   A cold-blooded vertebrate, such as lizards, snakes, and alligators, for example. The Cretaceous Period marked the peak of the reptiles' success with the dominance of the dinosaurs, which were reptiles.

REVOLUTION   The motion of one celestial body around another. The Moon revolves about Earth; the planets revolve around the Sun.

RIBOSOME   Those structures within a cell where the manufacture of protein takes place.

RNA (ribonucleic acid)   A nucleic acid that is important in the manufacture of protein in cells.

ROTATION   The motion of a body around its axis. The Sun and all of the planets rotate. Earth completes one rotation about every 24 hours.

SEDIMENTARY ROCK   Rock formed from clay, lime, sand, gravel—and sometimes plant and/or animal remains—that have been squeezed under great weight and pressure for long periods of time. Sedimentary rock makes up about 75 percent of the land area of the world. Sedimentary rocks, unlike igneous and metamorphic rocks, often contain fossils.

SEDIMENTS   The loose bits and pieces of clay, mud, sand, gravel, lime, and other earth materials that pile up century after century and become squeezed by the great weight of new sediments above. Eventually, such sediments heaps may be thrust up as new mountains.

SILURIAN PERIOD   That geologic time period in the Paleozic Era spanning some 40 million years and that lasted from 440 million years ago to 400 million years ago.

SOLAR SYSTEM   The Sun and its nine known primary planets accompanied by about 60 known satellites, plus many lesser objects, including comets, asteroids, meteoroids, and at least one planetoid.

SPECIES   Any one kind of animal or plant group, each member of which is like every other member in certain important ways. All populations of such a group are capable of interbreeding and producing healthy offspring.

SPONTANEOUS GENERATION   The erroneous belief that living things are created out of decaying meat, mud, dust or the like. The idea had supporters from at least the time of Aristotle until the French scientist Louis Pasteur put the notion to rest once and for all around 1800.

STARS Hot, glowing globes of gas that emit energy. The Sun is a typical, and our closest, star. Most stars are enormous compared with planets, containing enough matter to make thousands of Earthlike planets. Stars generate energy by the fusion of atomic nuclei in their dense and hot cores. Stars seem to be formed out of clouds of gas and dust, evolve through various stages, and finally end their lives as dark, cold objects called black dwarfs.

STROMATOLITES Dome-shaped fossil remains made up of hundreds of wafer-thin layers. These little mounds, found in western Australia, for instance, are the fossil remains of colonies of primitive bacteria. They are the oldest known fossils and are about 3.5 billion years old.

SUPERNOVA A giant star whose brightness is tremendously increased by a catastrophic explosion. Supernova stars are many thousands of times brighter than ordinary nova stars. In a single second, a supernova releases as much energy as the Sun does over a period of about 60 years.

SYMBIOSIS The act of two organisms living in association, each providing the other with one or more vital benefits.

TEMPERATURE A measure of how hot or cold a body is, "hotness" meaning the rate of atomic motion, or kinetic energy. The greater the kinetic energy, the "hotter" a substance is said to be.

TERTIARY PERIOD That geologic time period in the Cenezoic Era spanning 64 million years and that lasted from about 66 million years ago to 2 million years ago.

TRIASSIC PERIOD That geologic time period in the Mesozoic Era spanning about 50 million years and that lasted from some 245 million years ago to about 195 million years ago.

VARIATION The racial and certain other differences among the individuals making up a population. These variations are what lead to evolutionary change.

VERTEBRATE   Any group of animals having a backbone, which provides support and protects the nerves of the spinal cord.

WARM-BLOODED   Having a self-regulating body temperature. Warm-blooded animals, such as mammals, generate their own heat rather than depending on heat from the air or land, as cold-blooded animals (for example, reptiles) do.

WEATHERING   The erosion of rocks and soil by frost and other weather conditions. Small pieces of rock on mountains are continually being chipped off and carried away by the wind and streams as sediment particles, many of which are carried far out onto the ocean floors. Mechanical weathering is the physical breakdown of rock, for example, by frost. Chemical weathering is the chemical breakdown of rock by acid rain, produced naturally or by sulfur and nitrous pollutants released by factories.

WHITE DWARF   A very small star that radiates stored energy rather than new energy through nuclear fusions. The Sun is destined to become a white dwarf after it goes through the red-giant stage.

Further Reading

Cloud, Preston. *Oasis in Space* (Earth's history from the beginning). New York: W. W. Norton, 1988. (AR)

————. *Cosmos, Earth, and Man* (a short history of the universe). New Haven: Yale University Press, 1978. (AR)

Cole, Joanna. *The Human Body: How We Evolved* (an account of human evolution, punctuated by explanations of the development of specific parts of the human body). New York: Morrow, 1987. (ER)

de Beer, Sir Gavin. *Atlas of Evolution* (oversized picture atlas of evolution). New York: Nelson, 1964. (ER)

Dobzhansky, Theodosius. *Genetic Diversity and Human Equality* (the roles environment and genetics play in determining intelligence). New York: Basic Books, 1973. (AR)

ER = Easy reading
AR = Advanced reading

Eldredge, Niles. *Life Pulse* (episodes from the story of the fossil record). New York: Facts on File, 1987. (ER)

———. *Time Frames* (the rethinking of Darwinian evolution and the theory of punctuated equilibria). New York: Simon & Schuster, 1985. (AR)

Gallant, Roy A. *Ancient Indians* (the peopling of the Americas by Paleo-Indian cultures from 10,000 years ago and earlier). Hillside, N.J.: Enslow, 1989. (ER)

———. *Private Lives of the Stars* (the Big Bang, stellar evolution, and the black holes). New York: Macmillan, 1986. (ER)

———. *Earth's Changing Climate* (a history of climate change, the natural and human forces that alter climate, and how we may be setting the stage for future climate change). New York: Four Winds Press, 1979. (ER)

———. *How Life Began: Creation* versus *Evolution* (a review of the ongoing controversy between the creationists and evolutionary biologists). New York: Four Winds Press, 1975. (ER)

———. *Charles Darwin: The Making of a Scientist* (a short biography of Darwin and his idea of evolution through natural selection). Garden City, N.Y.: Doubleday, 1972. (ER)

Gastonguay, Paul R. *Evolution for Everyone* (what evolution is, what it may soon become, and how it ultimately affects us). Indianapolis: Bobbs-Merrill, 1974. (ER)

Lauber, Patricia. *Dinosaurs Walked Here and Other Stories Fossils Tell* (reconstructions of prehistoric events as revealed by the fossil record). New York: Bradbury Press, 1987. (ER)

Margulis, Lynn. *Early Life* (concentrates on the evolution of cells). Boston: Science Books International, 1982. (AR)

Margulis, Lynn, and Dorion Sagan. *Microcosmos* (4 billion years of evolution from our microbial ancestors). New York: Summit Books, 1986. (AR)

Moody, Paul A. *Introduction to Evolution* (a general introduction to evolution). New York: Harper & Row, 1970. (AR)

Osborn, Fairfield, ed. *Our Crowded Planet* (essays on the pressures of population). Garden City, N.Y.: Doubleday, 1962. (AR)

Pfeiffer, John E. *The Emergence of Humankind* (from the age of mammals to humans and their ascent up the cultural ladder of evolution). New York: Harper & Row, 1985. (AR)

Pringle, Laurence. *One Earth, Many People* (the challenge of human population growth). New York: Macmillan, 1971. (ER)

————. *The Only Earth We Have* (the necessity of treating the environment with respect). New York: Macmillan, 1969. (ER)

————. *Dinosaurs and Their World* (life, times, and extinction of the dinosaurs). San Diego: Harcourt Brace Jovanovich, 1968. (ER)

Sattler, Helen Roney. *Hominids: A Look Back at Our Ancestors* (an introduction to human evolution). New York: Lothrop, Lee & Shepard, 1988. (ER)

Seielstad, George A. *Cosmic Ecology* (from space geometry to prescriptions for surviving the dilemma created by cultural evolution). Berkeley: University of California Press, 1983. (AR)

Shapiro, Harry L. *Peking Man* (the mystery of the disappearance of the bones of Peking Man). New York: Simon & Schuster, 1974. (ER)

Simpson, George Gaylord. *The Meaning of Evolution* (a study of the history of life and of its significance for all of us). New Haven: Yale University Press, 1967. (AR)

Index

Italics indicate glossary entries.

PICTURE CREDITS: Title page, Peabody Museum of Natural History; pages 3 and 18, Palomar Observatory Photographs, Carnegie Institute of Washington; page 47, Carolina Biological Supply Company; page 54, courtesy Harriet Gallant; pages 63, 84, 115 (all), 141 (both), 143 (bottom), photos by Roy A. Gallant; page 66, National Park Service Photo by Richard Frear; pages 86, 99, 133 (bottom), 140, American Museum of Natural History, photos by Roy A. Gallant; pages 89 (Neg.#Geo80820), 93 (Neg.#Geo80821), 102 (Neg.#Geo80772), 118 (Neg.#Geo80874), 124 (Neg.#J.C.H.Geo80004), Field Museum of Natural History, Chicago; pages 96 (Neg.#322871), 101 (Neg.#322872, photo by Logan), 113 (Neg.#319836), courtesy Department of Library Services, American Museum of Natural History; page 104 (Neg.#CK73837), Field Museum of Natural History, Chicago, and the artist; page 116, drawing after M. Wilson; page 131, UPI/Bettmann Newsphotos.